As a Registered Nurse with a long career in Emergency Medicine, caring for every type of illness and injury known to man and caring for patients in such a high stress atmosphere was all she knew how to do.

It wasn't until after sustaining a life changing - career ending injuries in a freak accident herself, did she realize that being the patient brought a whole new meaning to pain, strength, motivation and hope. Having been through a medical life altering experience, it has given her a completely different perspective of how your life, your body, your mind, your finances change in an instant. Never take a moment for granted because you never know when life as you know it will change in a split second.

By using her medical and counseling career, combining it with her personal experience as a patient, she can help you take your own experiences and personal situations of adversity, and turn it around. She will give you examples, steps and true stories you can relate to in your own life. These stories will make you laugh, motivate you, bring you to tears and allow you to see that you are not alone in what you are going through. She has been there and understands how even the smallest of issues can feel like the end of the world, when you are experiencing it in real time. By reading this book, you will hear from someone who has been where you are and help guide you to where you want to be. It's not an easy road, but after working very hard herself, getting back up was the only option to move forward.

Shattered...

*Picking yourself back up when
your life is in pieces.*

Linda Frame, RN, CLNC, CCM

BALBOA.
PRESS

A DIVISION OF HAY HOUSE

Balboa Press books may be ordered through booksellers or by contacting:

Balboa Press
A Division of Hay House
1663 Liberty Drive
Bloomington, IN 47403
www.balboapress.com
1 (877) 407-4847

Because of the dynamic nature of the Internet, any web addresses or links contained in this book may have changed since publication and may no longer be valid. The views expressed in this work are solely those of the author and do not necessarily reflect the views of the publisher, and the publisher hereby disclaims any responsibility for them.

The author of this book does not dispense medical advice or prescribe the use of any technique as a form of treatment for physical, emotional, or medical problems without the advice of a physician, either directly or indirectly. The intent of the author is only to offer information of a general nature to help you in your quest for emotional and spiritual well-being. In the event you use any of the information in this book for yourself, which is your constitutional right, the author and the publisher assume no responsibility for your actions.

Any people depicted in stock imagery provided by Getty Images are models, and such images are being used for illustrative purposes only. Certain stock imagery © Getty Images.

Print information available on the last page.

ISBN: 978-1-9822-1724-2 (sc)
ISBN: 978-1-9822-1725-9 (hc)
ISBN: 978-1-9822-1723-5 (e)

Library of Congress Control Number: 2018914277

Balboa Press rev. date: 12/14/2018

To Erica Udeanu,
… for saving my life

Your powerful words of inspiration and your integrity pulled me
from a dark place after my accident and brought me back to life
again. I will be forever grateful. Thank you for your friendship.

Every adversity, every failure, every heartache carries with it the seed of an equal or greater benefit.

—Napoleon Hill

Contents

FOREWORD

We all have a story to tell, a unique voice with which to tell it, and an audience simply praying for us to tell it so that we might ease their pain, suffering, and despair.

I have always believed this to be true, but it wasn't until a series of events connected me with a physically and emotionally broken soul that I fully understood the divine truth of this.

I am an online business coach and mentor, and in the winter of 2014, I did something rather peculiar. I left the comfort of my home office to cut motivational and inspirational videos while standing in the snow.

This was a particularly cold winter, and temperatures had fallen to around negative thirteen degrees Fahrenheit. In most of the videos, my breath billowed out in soft puffy clouds as I spoke, and my lips would start to go numb and turn blue around the two-minute mark, so I kept these videos quite brief. I have no idea what inspired me to go out into the snow to record the videos, other than I felt called to do so.

Unbeknownst to me, on the other side of the world a once vibrant, energetic, and indomitable woman lay broken in her bed, one side of her body smashed into pieces from a horrific fall. She was unable to find the motivation, will, or desire to put her life back together.

She'd lost her job, the bills were piling up, her devoted and beloved fur baby of seventeen and a half years had just passed away, and she had slipped into a deep, dark pit of despair.

Here's where it gets interesting.

Linda was not familiar with Facebook, but for some reason felt called to check it out. And there, right before her eyes, was this crazy lady, freezing her face off in the snow.

What the heck is she doing? Linda thought.

And that was all it took for Linda to stop scrolling, hit play. and turn the sound up.

What happened next changed the course of Linda's life ... and mine.

Every day, Linda would tune into my videos, and over time we formed a connection. When I learned of her story, I asked her, "Have you ever thought about blogging?"

"What the heck is blogging?" she asked.

I explained to Linda that as she began to put the pieces of her life back together, she could help people overcome adversity, especially because of her extensive experience as a counselor and registered nurse.

A light bulb went off, and Linda Frame the blogger (and now, author) was born.

I have read every blog post Linda has ever written, and in so many of her posts, it seemed she was talking directly to me. Linda's gift is in knowing how to dissect any adversity—depression, unbearable grief, loss, separation, cancer, bullying, personal injury, overwhelming debt— and give the gentle guidance you need to steer yourself away from the darkness and into the light. She does so in such a way that you feel her message was crafted and tailored specifically for you. What you hold in your hands right now is a treasured gift—a gift of knowing that no matter what you're facing right now, you're going to be okay.

In this book, Linda will guide you to a profound understanding that every single adversity you are handed has within it the seed of a greater opportunity and a hint toward your true calling.

Who would have thought that Linda's physically, emotionally and financially devastating accident could hold within it the seed of something so life-changing, not just for Linda but for all of those who are fortunate enough to read Linda's message of genuine hope.

As you read through this book, I encourage you to "turn the sound up," and let Linda's message reach deep into your heart, tweak your soul into forward action, and perhaps even inspire you to turn your adversity into your own hero's journey.

Love and hugs,
—Erica Udeanu

PREFACE

How Did This Happen to Me?

You are about to hear the story of my adversity, pain, and struggle. Out of nowhere, my life changed in an instant, never to be the same, and I was forced to take the climb of a lifetime; I was tested beyond reason and endured pain that no one should ever experience.

If you have ever been tested by struggles, pain, loss, or anything that was out of your control, you will relate to this book. Anything can happen in a split second to change your world, and suddenly you are overwhelmed. Your cries of pain and search for help often go unanswered. Is this fair? Heavens no. Is it a test? It might be, but we'll never know while we are living on earth. Is it payback for something we did? I don't believe it is. Payback means getting what you have coming to you, something negative that you deserve, but no one deserves to suffer as I did—or as you may be suffering. Your payback will come in the afterlife; it is not judged in the present. No one on earth has that type of power over you or can control your outcome in that way.

Experiencing misfortune is an uncomfortable feeling, but whatever you are going through, you are not alone. I was raised to believe that "others are going through worse things than you are." This is true, but it's hard to remember that at the time of your traumatic event.

What is adversity? *Merriam-Webster* defines it as "misfortune," but adversity comes in a variety of ways—death, loss, pain, hurt, struggles, challenges, grief, and more.

This book is based on events that happened to me, including a devastating accident that changed my life in an instant. My intention with this book is to help you through your own struggles and show you how to find strength and courage in all areas of your life, as I did.

—Linda Frame

ACKNOWLEDGMENTS

Thank you to my brother, Neill Frame, and his wife, Pam, neither of whom gave up on me after my accident or throughout my long recovery. Your patience, kindness, giving, and positive support was unwavering. You helped with the many hospital and doctors' visits, as well as endless daily errands—grocery shopping, prescription pickups, taking out the garbage, blowing snow from my driveway—without my asking, even though your plate was already full at home. I will be forever grateful to you, Neill. You didn't help just because you're my brother but because that is who you are. I thank you from the bottom of my heart.

You are a wonderful man, a good husband, a good father, and the best brother. Your support has meant the world to me. During my recovery, you were my mind when I couldn't think, my voice when I couldn't find the words, my patience when I didn't have any, and my strength when I was at the end of my rope. You also stood by me when Workers Compensation insurance failed to cover me in those first four months. Thank you, Neill, for standing with me during that very scary time and fighting for me. I never could have done it without you. You truly are my rock.

Thank you to the one who truly believed in me from the time we met, convincing me that I had a story to tell—Erica Udeanu. One day after my horrific accident, I stumbled across your videos on the Internet, and I realized you were talking to me. Your words and messages of inspiration strengthened me and helped me to get up every morning and believe in myself again. After watching your video every day, I started to feel stronger and eventually went from overwhelming depression to feeling positive and motivated.

Today, I'm recovered and continue to be blessed with your and Alex's wonderful friendship. Erica, thank you for working with me and never giving up on me, although saying thank-you hardly seems enough for the strength you instilled in me to find my way back to what I know. You are an eloquent master of words and motivation.

Thank you to all of my online friends who believed in my ability to write. My EN Boot Camp family/colleagues have all been so supportive of my online business success. There were the combined efforts of blogging and video training, marketing, traffic, guidance and technical advice by Erica and Alex Udeanu. There were various stages of development, support and brainstorming from the members of the Totally Inspired Living Tribe (TILT) and from my EN Events Circle that kept me inspired on a daily basis.

The writings of Tony Robbins, Brendon Burchard, Napoleon Hill, Louise Hay, Jim Rohn, Wayne Dyer, and Joyce Meyer gave me additional inspiration, positivity, and belief I didn't know I had.

This book never could have come to life without the efforts of Hay House Publishing and Balboa Press, with the tireless staff within these incredible organizations.

Thank you to Lisa Wytrykus Kleppek for compiling all my scribbles and for being willing to do the copy-and-paste work with me.

Finally, thanks to Anna Urban of Anna Urban Photography for capturing my little buddy Lacey, my rescued four-legged furry bundle of joy that makes my heart smile every day. Anna, your patience and creativity of light, moments, and beautiful settings was absolutely amazing. You capture not just a picture but love between two beings that I believe only you could create. Anna, you made this experience comfortable, a joy, and just magical.

Most important, thank you to the two surgeons who put me back together—Dennis Andersen, MD, hand and upper extremity specialist of Aurora St. Luke's Medical Center, Milwaukee, who brought his surgical team to the out-of-town hospital where I was admitted and meticulously putting my right hand, arm, and especially my wrist back together again. Without his expertise, I would not have been able to write this book. And Paul Sienkiewicz, MD, knee and lower extremity specialist of Aurora St. Luke's, who gave me a total knee replacement and my lower extremity fractures care. Without his expertise, I would not be walking normally again. These two surgeons took on the challenges of my injuries and provided exceptional procedures when no one else could. In addition, thanks to all the nurses, physician assistants, nurse practitioners, and occupational and physical therapists, both inpatient and outpatient, as well as the two Customer Service Representatives of the Franklin Office, Judy and Lisa, for keeping me calm. *Thank you all from the bottom of my heart.*

INTRODUCTION

I wrote this book a year after experiencing a horrific accident. My injuries were extensive—I had fractures on my right side, fingers to elbow and ankle to thigh. I had three surgeries that gave me a totally new knee and a rebuilt wrist—these multiple fractures took a long time to heal. In addition, I had a considerable amount of nerve damage in my right hand that resulted in limited function—difficult because I was right-handed and unable to use my hand. After two weeks in the hospital, I was sent home—and that is when I realized how incapacitated I really was.

As a registered nurse, I spent most of my career working in the emergency room, which felt like a second home; that is where I was most comfortable in a hospital. I eventually transferred to the Urgent Care/Walk-In Department in the clinic, primarily because I felt it was time to slow down after a long run in the ER.

Prior to my accident, however, I'd had no experience in being a patient. I'd had outpatient procedures, but those resulted in a quick return to work and function. Spending two weeks in the hospital after my accident was not only new to me but scary because I had medical complications from my care that delayed the start of all required surgeries. After two long weeks in the hospital, I was finally sent home.

As I indicated, that's when I realized how badly injured I was. Being unable to care for myself, walk, or function on my own due was a very frustrating and lonely place to be. Thousands of things were roaring around in my head—what I needed or wanted to do, where I needed to be—but even getting something to drink or using the bathroom was a daunting, painful task that I dreaded and put off as long as I could.

Television was only entertaining for about five days at most; commercials often reminded me of fun things I couldn't do. Reading was difficult because I could use only my left hand and couldn't hold the book and turn pages without it dropping to the floor. Besides, reading and television just put me to sleep because of the pain medication I was on.

As the days and weeks progressed, my dog, Lexie, a rescue mix—primarily Australian cattle dog, corgi (with longer legs), and golden retriever—was brought home to me. The vet's office thought she was a little depressed from being away from me so long; she was unsettled, restless, and weak and wouldn't eat. Finally, on her second day back home, I slid down on the floor, and she immediately crawled on my lap and fell asleep. Getting up from the floor was a very difficult and painful ordeal, but for the next week, Lexie and I spend the nights on the floor like that, and she ate better. Eventually, I had to use my bed instead of the floor, and Lexie used her bed beside mine, and her routine resumed.

Two weeks after Lexie came home, I woke up one morning and realized Lexie was still sleeping and snoring. When Lexie didn't wake up and come when I called, I knew something was wrong. She was alive but unresponsive. I called my brother, who drove us to the vet's office. Sadly, Lexie never awoke and died. It was devastating to lose my best friend after seventeen and a half years with me.

Over the next week I became withdrawn, felt isolated, and didn't care about anything. I felt myself slipping further and further into a very dark, lonely place. This state of mind was uncharacteristic for me—actually, I didn't even realize I was in this dark place—and the only time I got up was for my home physical therapy and home occupational therapy appointments during the week. Other than that, I had little interest in anything. The mail kept coming, and the bills kept coming, but I had no money. I'd lost my job due to my injuries, but I couldn't do anything anyway. I just wanted to bury myself in a hole.

Many weeks went by, and then one day I opened my iPad—the first time since before my accident—and when I clicked on Facebook, I saw a video of a woman standing outside in the snow. It appeared very cold outside because I could see her breath as she spoke, so I turned up the volume and listened. It was a short video, but when it ended, I really didn't remember what she'd said, so I replayed it. This time it seemed as though, strangely, she was talking to me.

After I watched the video a second time, I noticed the comment section at the bottom of the screen—many people had commented on the video. I had no idea why the woman in the video was outside in the snow, talking to a camera. Was she some type of reporter? I only learned that her name was Erica Udeanu, and she was a New Zealand native, living in Bucharest, Romania. *What a lovely soothing accent she has*, I thought, *but who is she?*

For the next several weeks, I picked up my iPad when I woke up every morning and opened up Facebook—and that crazy lady in the snow was there like clockwork. I still couldn't figure out why she was there, but I listened every day, and she seemed to talk to me. After I listened to her video, I felt more inspired, positive, and motivated to get up and face the grueling task of the day. My therapists noticed marked improvements in my therapies, and I knew I was moving better. My determination was returning, and I felt stronger each day, all from feeding my mind with the positive, motivating, and supportive information I heard in Erica's video.

This transformation from being in a very dark, cold, and lonely place to becoming more inspired, energetic, motivated, and alert helped me to realize who I was as a person. I was a nurse who had spent her entire career helping people who were sick, injured, or dying—those who had been in accidents and were unable to care for themselves. I spent my career teaching and counseling patients to help themselves— encouraging, inspiring, and motivating them.

I wrote this book after writing hundreds of blogs and shooting videos online every day. I did these things as a result of my accident, as well as a result of what I have done in my entire nursing career. I did the blogs and videos from my heart for those who also face adversity and have been unable to find their way back.

I hope this book will resonate with you. I know what it's like to go through these things; I've been there. I hope my thoughts will inspire and motivate you and allow you to see how you too can pull yourself back up. A woman standing in the snow woke me up and made me realize who I really was. I hope I can help you with whatever you are going through. You are not alone because I am right here with you.

CHAPTER I

Adversities

We all go through occasional challenging times, but serious adversity or sudden life-changing events can deeply affect us and change us from who we were to who we are now. I hope that the stories in this chapter will help pull you back up from that life-changing moment.

I Have Never Felt So Alone

Have you ever experienced loneliness? I don't mean being alone; I mean true loneliness—a feeling so intense that you've said to yourself, "I've never felt so alone." Maybe the feeling was caused by the breakup of a relationship (either a lover or a friend), a divorce, or the death of a loved one. Think about that question again to be sure this subject really fits you and describes your level of loneliness. Then you will see the extreme level of this topic.

I am talking to those who have had an extreme end to something or someone in their lives—something or someone will never be there again. This extreme type of loneliness starts with the never-ending pain inside of you that is unbearable to the point that you cannot find any relief. You may have cried it out, or you may not have cried at all. Then you sit motionless for what turns out to be hours, not really hearing anything around you, not even thinking about anything in particular. You're just blank. You don't talk because you have nothing to say. You don't feel hot or cold, and you are unaware of anyone in the same room with you. Your body feels heavy, even your arms or legs, and it takes an enormous amount of energy to get up to use the restroom. When you do, you never notice the mirror, which others see as odd. You do not want the television on because the noise is too much, or the dopey commercials and happy shows are too painful to watch or hear. You just sit, without thoughts or words to say. You don't care to move; you feel blank. Some call this the "shock" period, but you know it as being numb. You may go for several days without eating because nothing appeals to you, and nothing tastes or smells like anything you recognize. (Honestly, you don't even think about eating.) You have lost any sense of priorities or responsibility because you cannot think straight; you do not even realize what day it is. You are just numb.

Obviously, everyone handles loneliness in his or her own way. There is no right or wrong way to handle it; there are no rules for what is healthy or not healthy. I want to talk to you about how to help yourself or others—maybe a friend or family member—who are going through this loneliness. I want you to understand it so you know what is happening to you. I feel if you understand loneliness and its symptoms or phases, you may find your way out of the lonely world you're in.

The pain that accompanies extreme loneliness is normal; it's your body and mind reacting to this sudden horrific event. Other things happen to you along the way—these are *phases* that help you separate the journey of loneliness. First, though, let's acknowledge this uncomfortable feeling you are having. Loneliness is pain, but this pain is unlike anything you've had with an injury or during an illness, like the flu. Loneliness is pain that affects you both physically and mentally, and it shows that you have something important to learn—but don't misunderstand me. I am not saying that the loss of a particular person (or anything else) occurred just so you could learn a lesson. Let's look at the various phases that occur and the painful experience of loneliness.

Everyone goes through the different phases of loneliness in his or her own way. The first phase is often *withdrawal*. This phase can take a few different directions. You may physically escape or seclude yourself away from everyone so you don't have to talk, and you can be without noise. But then the silence is smothering, a constant reminder that your special person is *really gone*. You find that you're unable to concentrate because it's too quiet. You're unable to concentrate because you're becoming restless. Television or reading is now boring. You want to do something, but what do you want to do? You finally move around, trying to do something, but your attention span is less than five minutes.

Finally, after being secluded for so long, you move in another direction or busy yourself to keep your mind occupied, moving on autopilot, doing things you have never done. You keep yourself active with constant work and long hours, doing something every night after work and going out late with groups of people you never cared for before, but you are filling in the time with constant activities. You've gone from seclusion to nonstop activities. What is going on? You are running away from yourself, you are running away from the loneliness, and you are running away from having to go home to emptiness and the reality of your life. You have been spending this phase of your withdrawal keeping busy so you don't have to think or remind yourself of your loneliness because that person is gone.

This busy phase has no time frame; it varies depending on the intensity of your particular loneliness. Some keep busy to help them cope; others keep busy to keep from falling apart if they find themselves with too much time on their hands. We each have our own reasons, unknown to us at the time, but we eventually get tired and realize we are running away from our loneliness. As we start to slow down, this point is when we enter the phase of *aloneness*.

Aloneness is finally developed when you are comfortable with yourself. You have developed your inner personality and resources that give you new thoughts, interests, and activities, as well as a new attitude that actually makes you comfortable when alone with yourself.

How did you get to this phase of aloneness? You had a long struggle of loneliness, pain, withdrawal, seclusion, numbness, and restlessness. You ran away from yourself and avoided going home. You now can accept loneliness and aloneness by becoming more comfortable in being alone with yourself.

Here's where the pain of loneliness offers something important to learn. By accepting loneliness, you also accept that loneliness has healing qualities. The period when you were alone allowed you to develop your inner self—self-growth, self-reflection, and self-examination. All the emptiness and hollowness you felt were replaced by inner strength. You made a huge step toward independence when you became comfortable being by yourself and no longer depended on the company of others.

There's enormous therapeutic value in being by yourself and being lonely for a while. Time really is the best healer of loneliness. That painful period of loneliness is a necessary part of the remedy you need to find yourself, to find out who you are, and to find out that you can be comfortable with being alone. This whole process of loneliness helps you to grow and to find the balance between being alone and being with others. You have a new personality, new growth, and new strength you've never had before. *You are now a survivor.*

Overcoming Discouragement

Being overcome with discouragement can affect your daily life. You can't think straight. You get overwhelmed with daily tasks, like paying the bills, rent or mortgage, and utilities. Most of the time you don't even want to get out of bed. You thinking, *I just don't want to go there.*

Some folks will look at this avoidance as denial, but you actually don't know where to start because you are so overwhelmed. You feel so smothered in your low emotional state that you can't sort out your priorities. You can't find your way out of the fog.

Let me give you three things to think about—this may be two more than you want to consider, but you'll have them for later as the fog clears:

- Write

Just write out your feelings. You have emotions trapped inside you, and they increase your level of being down and discouraged. When you get them out by writing them down, you actually release that internal pressure.

Write about whatever has you down. For example, write about your grief, loss, stress, anger, confusion, or anything else that's bothering you.

- Surround

You need to surround yourself with positives—positive, uplifting music; positive and encouraging examples in books or on television documentaries; and positive people. Stay away from all negatives—news reports, depressing music, negative television and books, and certainly negative people.

Positives initially will distract you from your overwhelming feelings. The positives will then help you to feel better, and as you start feeling better, your "down" emotions and discouragement with start to lose their grip on you.

- Listen

Start listening to the way you talk to yourself. If you're saying or thinking negative things about yourself, your situation, or your future, you are only pulling yourself back down.

Be aware of what you're saying, and speak of only positive things. Then start believing them. Laugh at your mistakes, and start loving yourself. If you don't change your outlook from deep inside, your projected external attitude will never change.

Difficult times always create opportunities for you to experience more love in your life.

Are You Overreacting When Things Fall Apart?

Here are examples of how to handle setbacks:

After I had a total knee replacement, the immobility and pain were constant reminders of how limited I was. I was already compromised from the rebuilding of my hand and arm, so I was a mess—and I still have a long way to go. Whenever I dropped something or couldn't reach an item or even when something just went wrong, how I reacted to it was so very important.

If you're already down, don't add to it by immediately reacting hatefully and negatively. When something does not go as planned, don't say, "This is horrible. My life is ruined."

Many of us have said those words. Stop doing that to your mind. Don't overreact to the present moment. Do a better job of remembering that unpleasantness will happen, but it also will go away.

Don't continue to put yourself down when there's a setback. Catch yourself when you start thinking negatively about the situation. Then ask yourself, "What can I learn from this? How can I become wiser and/or stronger from this?"

Don't dwell on what just fell apart. Restructure the negative episode, and build a positive outcome that will provide a stronger result.

Think before you react. Sure, it's hard to do, but don't feed your mind with anything but positive strength.

> *Sometimes good things fall apart so better things can fall together.*

Why Does Everything Have to Go Wrong?

I am a career-long Registered Nurse (RN) and spent most my career working in the emergency room and the trauma unit. I stayed there for so many years because my work as an RN came from my heart and not my bank account. (Frankly, there isn't enough money in the world to pay someone for the work of an RN). Now I have phased out of ER but still do some Clinic work. My passion, however, has been refocused on helping others in a different way.

After my accident and two-week hospital stay, I still faced a very lengthy recovery and rehabilitation. I mention this so you'll know that I understand what someone faced with adversity is going through.

As well as being an RN, I'm also an entrepreneur—a business owner. So what does an entrepreneur and a nurse who had an accident have to do with you? As I've indicated, I hope to share encouragement through my words, which I hope will speak to your heart and soul, as I write about things we generally do not share with our families, our spouses, our children, or even our best friends.

I speak only from my heart through who I have become as a person and from the adversities I have faced in life. I speak from my heart as a nurse who has witnessed the adversities that individuals have gone through. I speak from my heart as a patient who has faced adversities daily. I also speak as an entrepreneur who has made and grown very successful businesses, from an embarrassing and humiliating negative bank balance into a lucrative lifestyle no one ever thought I could do by myself.

Now I want to share something we've all said at one time or another (some of us have said this a lot): "Why does everything have to go wrong?"

Yes, why *does* everything seem to go wrong? You might have a great few days, and then *bam!* You're knocked down for some reason. Now what? Do you just sit there and complain that you can never catch a break? Or say, "Why me? Why can't anything ever go right?" It takes a lot of energy and motivation out of you, doesn't it? You were on a roll when all of a sudden the rug got pulled right out from under you. Now what do you do? How do you handle these situations? Do you get up and start again, continue on, or just say, "Forget it. I'm done. I'm not doing this anymore. It's not worth it. I'm too broke. I'm hurt. I lost everything. Nobody cares." The list of excuses and complaints is endless, but it may be more appropriate to ask yourself why it happened in the first place.

The reality is that everyone goes through adversity—challenges, hard times, misfortune, bad luck, hardships. It's never timely, and in fact, it may seem to follow you around. Challenges will happen in life, most of which you have no control over. That answers the question of why it happened in the first place. So that leaves the question of how are you going to handle it?

Many people have a very rough time when things suddenly become a crisis. In the sports world, it's called "choking" or that the pressure got to them. I am a golfer, and like golfers who play the hometown course, I do very well with my buddies when there is nothing at stake. But if I were to play in a tournament, the pressure might get to me, and I might play poorly. Professional golfers, even though they get used to the pressure, also have bad days or even a bad week. Professional baseball players are similar to golfers in that respect, and many times their poor performance is referred as "choking" when they drop fly balls. Those days happen when even the player feels like he couldn't catch a ball the size of a beach ball.

It may not be an athlete who "chokes"; it may be a speaker who suddenly can't talk in front of an audience. He or she becomes tongue-tied. Or a salesman, during a presentation or sales pitch, suddenly can't remember the name of the product or even the company he works for.

Not everyone stumbles under pressure, of course. Some people thrive under pressure. You may have heard of the "anchor" in sports, known for coming through when you need him or her. There's a pinch hitter in baseball who's sent in when there's a situation on the line for the game. Most team sports have those types of positions and/or people who are specifically in a position because they thrive under pressure. The corporate world has the same pressure-hungry folks who work better, get more done, or are more creative when they are under pressure. Whatever the situation, those who can handle it when the chips are down generally are not born that way; it's not a hereditary trait. So why do some people handle pressure and adversity better than others? It is actually not a secret; it's a learned behavior.

The studies on this are endless, and you can spend a lot of time reading various theories, but I only want to address you and me.

I too have had many opportunities to take the "why me?" road. Consider my true story—a startling series of events with a tragic beginning. This story will show you another example of how you can take massive action or how having a positive mind-set affects outcome when the life you once knew it is suddenly turned upside down. This story also will show the different roads you can take when adversity puts you in that position of "Now what?"; "Why me?"; "Why now?"; "What can I do now?"; and of course, "Why does everything have to go wrong?"

Things only go wrong, if you let it ...

Nothing Is Going to Happen to Me

Life doesn't always happen the way you planned it.

Sure, you may take a step back or two that causes you to be late or that hands you more work than you expected. Sometimes, however, life takes an unexpected turn that throws you totally off guard. This unexpected obstacle is a bit different and most likely is something you've never experienced before.

Sometimes it takes a life-changing setback for you to truly understand the meaning of life. Until that life-changing devastation happens to you, you don't understand how much you take for granted. Until you experience that devastation, whether physical, emotional, or both, you may not understand the value of life.

How well do you understand? You may experience

- joy—until you face sorrow;
- faith—until it is tested;
- peace—until you are faced with conflict;
- trust—until you are betrayed;
- love—until it's lost;
- hope—until you are confronted with doubt;
- courage—until you have to get back on your feet;
- belief—until you've had to depend on your own;
- perseverance—until it was all up to you; or
- life—until yours has changed forever.

Remember, if you are facing devastation, loss, depression, or physical or emotional challenges, and now you feel like you can't get back up … you can and will.

Yes, I *do* understand because I have been there. I too have hit bottom after a devastating accident. I too have had to start over, physically, emotionally, and financially.

Was it easy for me? No it was not. It was the hardest thing I've ever done in my life.

I want you to understand four things:

- Do *not* take your life for granted.
- Do *not* assume tomorrow will be here.
- Do *not* think you are alone.
- Do *not* ever give up.

Adversities in life will make you stronger, smarter, and full of character—*if* you handle your climb back up with gratitude and humility. Don't wait until something happens to you to understand and be grateful for your life. Use each moment and each day to understand the true meaning of life, and *never* take tomorrow for granted.

> *Challenges are what make life interesting; overcoming them is what makes life meaningful.*

Are You Drowning and Overwhelmed?

When you are already down, feeling like the world is still coming down around you, you may become frozen. This happens for all types of challenges: grief, work issues, not having a job, recovering from an illness or injury, depression, lack of confidence or self-esteem, and so on. I heard from someone recently who is going through this. She said, "I just can't. I can't handle it anymore."

Whatever the issue, you first need to stop thinking—yes, stop thinking—about all that is weighing you down. Stop pulling more and more negative thoughts on top of you because you are already suffocating.

Breathe. Breathe. *Breathe.* Just empty your mind and focus on nothing but breathing. Only think about you. Pull your shoulders down and breathe slowly for two minutes; just do this. Let go of any other thoughts. Just breathe.

For today, you're only going to focus on you. Get something to drink and eat. Take care of only you. If you have children, ask for their help. Your children want to help you take care of you. Remember: today is only going to be about you. It's about getting you calmer and focusing on yourself. In order for whatever is weighing on your shoulders to fall off, you have to focus only on you.

You are taking a personal day, a day off, a *me* day. You have to let all that garbage fall off your shoulders before you drown in it—this is mandatory. You cannot handle challenges until you have strength within yourself. If it takes one or two days or more, so be it. When you are ready, then the key is handling only one challenge at a time. This is not the time for multitasking. If you don t handle only one issue at a time, you will feel like you're drowning again and again.

Strength comes from within. If you don't give yourself the time to obtain that strength, you will never get that mess off your shoulders. Think very wisely and work out this process carefully. Then you will be able to handle issues one at a time.

> *Have patience with all things but first of all with yourself.*

Do Your Words and Actions Match?

Getting home from the hospital after major surgery from life-changing injuries was an adventure in itself. I had a lot of visitors—many wonderful people who did things for me—and I saw people who I hadn't seen for a while. It also gave me a different perspective on many things that hadn't struck me before.

In one of the groups that came by to wish me well, I zeroed in on something that some of the folks may not have noticed. I saw it very clearly.

After going through life-changing injuries, multiple surgeries, and daily rehab and recovery rituals, I realized I'd changed. I was looking at and hearing things differently than I had before the accident. I had a different sense of life. I was more patient. I listened better and talked less. My life goals were crystal clear. Being stronger as a person, after all I went through, my listening to others and my observations are also quite different. I now see whole packages of interactions between people differently than I used to do.

Here is an example:

While I was home in rehabilitation and recovering from surgeries, I had visitors that would frequently stop by. On one particular day, a couple I knew that had been together for quite some time, stopped by stating they just wanted to keep me company, find out how I was doing, seeing if they could help and keep me relaxed. However, before long they began having an aggressive conversation between themselves which progressed into an argument. The atmosphere in the room suddenly became tense and I was very uncomfortable. At one point I thought to myself, I never realized before how petty people can be with one another.

The way you treat people says a lot about who you are. Be careful. Your actions are screaming over your words.

Your actions speak louder than your words.

How to Be Positive When Your Life Just Became Negative

When my life took a very unexpected turn, I went from a positive world to a negative within seconds. I'll share with you how I handled the obstacles and why. I'm not sharing this story to elicit pity; I'm sharing this in the hope of helping those in similar situations, so you know that you are not alone.

In addition to my being a full-time nurse, I also worked a second part-time job. This was my "fun" job that helped with the bills. I was a licensed bartender on a large excursion boat on our beautiful lake here in Lake Geneva, Wisconsin. I also had a third job as a legal nurse consultant, for which I worked with attorneys on medical cases, as needed. I enjoyed the balance in my life, of these three professions that utilized my experience and skills. I loved to stay busy, and I *was* busy every day of the week.

On September 5, 2014 I was at my "fun" job. I began the preparation for the bar setup with one of the essentials—ice. As I stepped in the large ice room, my life as I knew it changed in an instant. I found myself half lying and half sitting on the floor, and I felt the most horrific pain I'd ever experienced. Doctors often ask you what your pain level is, ranking it from one to ten. Honestly, on that scale, mine was at least forty-eight.

I looked at my legs, and the right one was in different directions. I knew that wasn't right. I instinctively reached out with my left hand and realigned my right leg. The horrific pain got worse, and I realized my right arm and hand were behind me. I pulled my right hand and arm around me and saw my hand hanging from my arm. I knew it wasn't supposed to hang like that, nor was my arm supposed to look like it did. My quick assessment was that nothing about my right hand, wrist, and arm looked right at all. I instinctively put immediate support under my hand, wrist, and forearm with my left hand.

I yelled for help (and muttered some expletives). Help came immediately, and then the next days were pretty fuzzy. First, there were a lot of people—the voices of those trying to help me when I fell—and everything seemed to move in slow motion until I heard a familiar voice at my left ear. It was my brother. At that moment, I was hearing in present time again.

He told me, "Linda, it's bad. It's really bad." That confirmed my opinion as a nurse, but it was good to have another opinion.

But why was my brother there? He also worked at the cruise line on the lake. He was the captain of the mail boat and was just getting ready to back the boat out for the mail-jumping tour when the office notified him of my fall. I appreciated his calm, reassuring voice and his honesty. but I knew the "mail must go through" and be on time when delivered on the lake to the piers.

After he left, the fuzzy journey started again. There was the ambulance ride to the hospital; stopping to get paramedics for severe pain medications; the emergency room with seemingly an eternity of waiting; IVs; x-rays (a lot of them); and hospital admission. I don't remember too much of except a lot pain, and the next several days were a blur.

I spent two weeks in the hospital. I had fractures in my right leg, right hand, and right forearm and wrist. A wonderful hand specialist, who came down from Milwaukee with his team, performed trauma surgery.

As I've mentioned, once I was home by myself, reality set in. I could have followed the "Why me?" road signs and turned down that road, but I did not—because I realized that I could not. Why? Well, I am not a superwoman, but I had to make a choice. I had to choose whether to play the "woe is me" sympathy card—I couldn't walk and couldn't use my dominant hand/arm—or to choose to heal.

When everything was going against me, why would I decide to be strong and take action? I had to do it. I was self-supporting. I owned a home with a mortgage. I had home utility bills. I had a car. I also had a wonderful elderly dog (17.5 years old) with a serious medical disorder that required daily care. I had many other expenses, and tragically, I lost not just one but all three of my income-producing jobs. This was a workers compensation injury because it happened at work, so I should have been compensated for being laid up and unable to work, but it wasn't that easy. I didn't realize I was facing the first of many hurdles I would have to scale.

As it turned out, the bills kept coming in, and by the second month after the accident, I still had not received anything from workers compensation. You may know that by the end of the second month of not paying any bills or the mortgage, the phone starts ringing off the hook. As the bills continued to flood in, I became so emotionally overwhelmed that I retained an attorney to handle workers compensation issues. Medical bills went unpaid, and the mortgage and other bills were now three months overdue. I still was unable to get around, and then, the most tragic situation occurred: my precious dog, Lexie, died. Lexie was my one constant, a reliable and unconditionally loving being. Bless her heart; at seventeen and a half years old, she couldn't hold on any longer. My world at that moment just went black.

Everyone has issues, hurdles, and unexpected things happen to them, and some things seem to explode all at once and change their lives. Big or small doesn't matter because when it happens to *you*, it's big. Why is it when something goes wrong, it keeps going wrong and presents more and more hurdles? You reach the point where you don't want to get up; you *can't* get up. (Why get up when something else will just go wrong?)

Let's recap my situation: the accident happened, resulting in multiple injuries, surgery, and a long hospital stay. I lost all three jobs because I was unable to work or get around and was having trouble caring for myself. I received calls from the mortgage company and my creditors because workers compensation wasn't paying me. I couldn't pay bills. I couldn't buy food. Medical bills kept piling up—workers compensation was not paying me *or* the medical bills. I needed additional surgery after complications arose from the first ones, so there were even more medical bills. Both surgeons said I would need more surgeries and would be out of work for eight months to a year. I hired attorneys, which added to my expenses to owe. My dog died.

You may have gone through similar adversity yourself and know what it's like. So what in the world do you do when you're in a situation like this? *You make a decision. You make a choice. You take action.*

We all have choice our lives. We can choose to cry and be negative, or we can choose to get up and make something happen—a positive action. Even when life changes in an instant, there comes a point when you must decide what needs to be done and how you will do it (what resources do you have left?). This awareness, which some call "taking assessment," is taking responsibility for yourself. Remember that you can be negative, or you can surround yourself with positive-minded, encouraging people; absorb their positive energy; and make the decision to take massive action—for yourself and by yourself.

You have to stand strong while going through the struggles of life— "hang in there," as the saying goes. Surround yourself with positives. Fill your life with positive people, positive music, positive books, and positive situations. Stay away from negative people; let them go. Positives make you feel better, and as you feel better, depression loses its grip on you.

When you're down, take a long honest look at your life as you knew it before the incident happened that changed your life. Were you happy? Are you happy now? Are you doing in life the things that make you smile and laugh, and you can't wait to get your day going? If not, then ask yourself why—why are you doing what you don't want to do? Why are you working somewhere that makes you miserable? That is not living your life. You only have one shot at life, and this is it. So if you're not happy where you are, or you're not happy while doing the job you have, ask yourself why.

You have to fight through the bad days in order to earn the best days; it's hard but worth it. You have to also believe that you *will* make it to the other side of this hardship, this adversity. One day you will look back with much wiser eyes and deeper understanding, as well as with much gratitude because of all you have learned and from which you have grown. Make a choice in your life. Live your passion in your life. Do not put it off because your life can change in an instant.

Working hard for something we don't care about is called stress. Working hard for something we love is called passion

17

How Are You Handling Your Issues?

At this very moment, something unexpected is going on or has happened in your life. No one is immune to incidents or misfortunes.

An outside force likely has given you a wrong answer, dealt you a bad deal, caused something to not work out the way you had hoped, taken away the things you like the most, changed your life in an instant, or taken away someone who was your best friend or the love of your life. Life can be so uplifting and glorious or so very cruel and unfair. Most of us have felt these rough waters at some time and have been scared.

So what are you supposed to do now when the cruel effects of life have rocked your word?

Give yourself some time alone first.

Next, spend time with and listen to others—those you trust the most.

Finally, give yourself time alone again to absorb and sort out everything that has happened, to understand the facts and the reality, to recall the words of wisdom given to you, and especially to consider your personal thoughts in regard to your situation.

You must give yourself alone time, listening time, and alone time again to absorb and sort things out in order to get back up. If you don't go through this process, the healing and moving forward processes will be compromised.

My life-changing accident left me with daily challenges, disappointments, pain, suffering, and eventually the tragic news of what I would have to live with as a result of my injuries.

"So what did you do after the accident"?. After the initial shock, however, I came around to the reality of what happened. Although it was difficult, I made up my mind that I could do this, that I *had* to do this because no one could do it for me. Family and friends were there; everyone comforted me, did what they could for me, and shared their love and concern. As much as they wanted to do things for me and help, however, there were things that only I could do myself.

So how did I know what to do? I didn't know because I was just as scared as my family and friends were. After I was left with the results of what the accident had done to me and the physical devastation, I realized that I had to make my own decisions. I knew what was wrong, I knew what was coming, and I knew I had to take responsibility for myself. I made up my mind to stop the negative—stop the pity party, stop the "I can't," stop the "poor me" and "what am I going to do now?" I had to take responsibility for what went in my mind and what came out—my mind-set—immediately.

Pain is a fact of life and an experience of hurt.

Suffering is feeling powerless to stop the pain.

Mind-set is to know and believe in your mind that you can get through your situation; to know and believe that you can visualize your positive results; to know and believe you have the commitment to make it through this issue successfully, whatever it is and with whatever it takes.

First, however, you have to do two things:

1. Believe in yourself. Know that you can get through the issues, whatever they are, successfully and as a better, stronger person.
2. Take action. Start to move forward toward getting back on your feet.

To get yourself back up, follow the following very easy formula to change your mind-set:

*   Know that you have massive potential to overcome whatever you're going through.
*   Believe that you are going to get through whatever you're going through.
*   Take massive action to keep yourself moving forward.
*   Visualize the results of your actual ability and potential, your belief in yourself to do it, your action to move yourself forward, and the results you are working toward.

Regardless of what's happened to you, remember where to start: (1) spend time alone; (2) spend time listening to those you trust; and (3) spend time alone again to absorb and sort out what's happened to you.

After you have completed the initial three steps, you'll be ready to start the four steps of mind-set.

Motivational speaker Tony Robbins is the master of mind-set for personal development. I encourage you to follow him; you won't regret it.

"Make it so today is not like yesterday, and tomorrow will be different forever".

—Tony Robbins

I Am So Down and Don't Know What to Do!"—How to Heal Yourself

I understand how hurt you are, how miserable and down you've been, and how it feels. I've been there myself.

But I want you to think about a few things that I am going to share with you—these thoughts helped me when I was going through a horrific time. I want you to understand that I had similar feelings to yours now, but I read and listened to some things that kept me going and moving toward getting back up.

You might think I have no clue about what you're going through, but you'd be wrong. I'm sharing these thoughts with you exactly because I have been there. The things that have hurt you, broken your heart, or made you cry with pain, grief, and even rage are the same things that have made you more human and more compassionate. When you have gone through these situations yourself, survived them, and made a complete turnaround, you are better able to help lift others. You might not realize or feel that now, but if you make yourself move forward, you will understand because you will have that power.

We heal and get stronger faster by helping others, by giving ourselves hope and believing in ourselves. The one thing we all desperately need and the most significant life-changing gift we can offer others is hope.

Most of the interesting, compassionate, and influential people in the world have faced major disappointments. These outstanding leaders have had their hearts broken more than once. They hear and march to a different drummer and have experienced devastating loneliness, despair, and failure. Not surprisingly, these are the same people who create beautiful art, music, dance, and theater; the same people who have become deeply intuitive, generous, and unconditionally accepting. They did not get back up through the power of money because they didn't have any. They found their way back up from their devastating experiences of hurt and loss, as I did, one step at a time.

I've can't emphasize enough how important it is for you to stop and think and to remember what I am about to share with you right now.

How to Heal Yourself

- Stop mentally abusing yourself.
- Stop agonizing over your past mistakes and worrying about the future.
- Calm your anxiety. Life is hard enough without added fear, panic, and anxiety.
- Your heart and soul is crying out for love and encouragement. Listen to it, and start feeding it with ideas of what you can do for yourself.
- Don't wait for someone to rescue you. Only you can do this, but it's easy to do. It's free, and you can start today.
- Breathe deeply, get present, and show compassion for yourself.
- Treat yourself well. Pamper yourself and take care of yourself because no one can do that but you.
- Realize that true happiness lies within you.
- Don't waste your time and energy looking outside for peace, contentment, and joy; it only comes from within you.
- There is no happiness in having or receiving; there is only happiness in giving.
- Don't believe that if you buy something for yourself you will feel better. That is selfish and will only make you feel worse by spending money.

You can do so many things to make yourself feel better inside:

- Find a way to give of yourself to others.
- Reach out to others.
- Share with others.
- Hug others.
- Help others.
- Make people smile or laugh. Make *their* day, not yours. Give others a thumbs-up and a smile; watch their smiles appear.
- Make someone's heart smile; yours will too.

When you give to others, you will feel one hundred times better in your heart and soul, and it will make their day.

> *"Be helpful. When you see a person without a smile, give them yours."*
>
> —Zig Ziglar

Do You Really Know about Bullying?

Unless you have been a victim of bullying, you couldn't know what it's all about.

Bullying is harsh, abrasive, hurtful, painful, terrorizing, and a daily nightmare and never-ending hell. How do I know? I was a victim of bullying for seventeen years, and the description of bullying that I just gave above don't even scratch the surface in describing the hell victims go through every day.

I grew up in a wonderful family—very loving. We were all very close and would rather be home together than anywhere else in the world. We did everything together as a family, including fun activities, fishing, waterskiing, travel, and even work. My father started my interest in woodworking and refinishing when I was in the first grade, which led to my formal training and to my work on boats and furniture today.

Living in a tourist town, where people from all over came to vacation and enjoy our beautiful, clear, spring-fed lake, meant the city was always busy and fun with bustling activity.

Many of us remember joyful, carefree, safe days growing up, when no one even locked their doors, and we all trusted each other, and we knew everyone.

One spring day during my fourth-grade year, I was enjoying the outdoors and the beauty of this awesome city. My days were carefree, but suddenly, this particular day became a day that I will never forget. Unbeknownst to me, a new neighbor boy—someone I didn't know—had been watching me, like a bird of prey watching his next meal source.

On this day, the boy, Johnny, he called himself, approached me to invite me to a "cool new place" he'd found that was "out back," in another neighbor's yard. Unnerved by his invitation, since all my neighbor friends and I played everywhere, I followed him with interest. We all looked to explore new spots to play.

Johnny led me to an old shed out in a field. I looked around and thought, wow my other neighborhood friends would love this place.

While I looked around with excitement, my imagination was working like a train engine, thinking about all the fun stuff my neighborhood friends and I could do there in our new fun place. We could climb, jump, swing, build, and gather. What a cool place, I thought. This new kid Johnny was right, it's a neat place.

During my careful examination of this "cool place" with its bright interior—the sun was shining in so brightly—it suddenly changed, and this cool new place suddenly became dark and cold. The sunshine that had warmed the room with its bold stream of light was gone. When I turned around, I noticed that Johnny had shut the rickety door and blocked the door from the inside so no one else could get in, and then he came over to me.

In my adolescent innocence, I had no idea why he'd shut the door. I had never known anyone who acted as he did then—forcefully with his voice serious, mean, and bossy. That was the first day of being sexually molested by a stranger, a neighbor, a bully who threatened me from that day on.

At that moment, the joyous, warm glow of sunshine that had illuminated the day was not the only thing that went dark. I felt a dark, terrorizing, painful fear that I had never experienced. It was at that moment that my beautiful, shining innocence—my carefree and trusting view of the world—was changed and never would be the same again.

For anyone who has been the victim of an act of violence, assault, or verbal inappropriateness, bullying doesn't stop. Once it's started in any manner—unless it's swiftly reported to someone in authority—it will continue indefinitely. For me, it continued throughout my grade school and high school years. Even beyond college, when I returned home to visit, Johnny would somehow find me, and the bullying would continue, I was constantly threatened though it was verbal bullying then.

Why didn't I walk away, say no, or tell my parents, brothers, or someone else I trusted? It doesn't work that way—not for me; not for anyone. Bullies are predators, and they have all the power over their victims. Their victims are physically and mentally smothered by fear, embarrassment, humiliation, and intimidation. Bullies have complete control over their victims, the threats are deafening every second of the day, and the victims' silence is demanded or else!

I had this ongoing secret that I could never tell. I was never free. I felt as though I was terrorized every day. My family never knew—no one ever knew—what was happening to me every day, for years and years to come. What I thought was just bullying, I realized later was actually was sexual assault. I was powered by someone, and I could not get away from him or find a way out. When he wasn't around, and I was in the privacy of my own home, this secret was always with me; I felt smothered by fear and intimidation. Why? Because Johnny drilled into my mind daily that he would easily find out if I told anyone, and then his next acts of his sexual torture would be worse. Victims of any age know only the smothering instructions they are given and that are reinforced every day; they do not know how to get free.

Even after Johnny's death, which I read about a few years ago in the obituaries of the local paper, the sexual assaults were never forgotten— nor will it ever be. Even today, I am still reminded of those terrorizing years, and it escalates when I drive by my childhood house and his.

Bullying is verbal, emotional, terrorizing, but sexual assault is physical, and so much more than anyone can ever imagine. This individual who started one day with being a bully, sexually assaulted me and followed me through college, at which point his ongoing abuse became verbal intimidations and threats.

Johnny eventually moved on, but I shuddered to think of other children he contacted after me. I could have prevented others from being sexually assaulted in the future if I'd said something, but as a child, I didn't know what to do. However, as adult I was still too terrified of him to ever speak of it. I knew I was alone and decided to keep to myself. Forever.

I still am haunted every day by his disgusting actions, threats and abuse and the fact I was not able to prevent him from harming anyone else after me. That was wrong of me to never say anything, but after the days, weeks months and years, I felt it was too late.

Never keep bullying, abuse, sexual assault to yourself, get help immediately!

If you are a victim or suspect someone is being bullied, act on it. Don't keep your thoughts to yourself.

> *If something feels off, it usually is. Walk away & get help*

CHAPTER 2

Attitude

Everyday life affects our decisions, actions, and often our personalities. Many of us do not realize that our attitudes are directly affected by what happens around us unless, we are conscious of how others perceive us. Being aware of our attitudes and how others see us is the key to getting along with others.

How to Deal with What You Cannot Control

"It's so annoying. I just wish they would stop doing that!"

How many times have you heard a similar statement? Little things set us off—things that others say or how something looks. We've all seen or heard things that we didn't like, even in a small way.

Believe it or not, not everything is done to upset us! We may know that, rationally, but so many times we forget, don't we? Instead of avoiding someone, getting irritated at every little thing, and walking away from something or someone you care for, do something different. Start thinking about things differently. There is only so much you can control, and that is really only yourself. I am going to a few thoughts on the difference between what you can and cannot control.

You cannot control another person's annoying habits, but you *can* do something about your own.

You cannot control the length of your life, but you *can* control its width and depth.

You cannot control the distance your head is above ground, but you *can* control the height of the contents you feed into it.

You cannot control the contour of your face, but you *can* control your expression.

You undoubtedly will come across someone you find a little "different" than everyone else. That's okay. It's not your responsibility to change anyone to suit you. Manage and control yourself well and be aware of your nonverbal responses. Also be aware of the content you put into your mind and how much learning you accept. Recognize your own habits and how you take care of your body. If you expend your energy on productive things, such as taking care of yourself and your business, what others do or say will be of no difference to you.

Use your energy wisely and make sure your actions are healthy, wholesome, positive, and pure. Live your life to the fullest. Be kind, not critical, of others, because you have no idea what another person is going through.

Change your thoughts, and you change your world.

Who cares about What I Do?

The answer to that question is … everyone.

Everything you do affects those around you. Everything you say affects those around you. If you're not aware of these simple facts, you should be, because all your actions and words have considerable effects on everyone.

The power of the word is massive. It can help or destroy someone before you take your next breath. The things you do can be equally powerful. Your actions can help someone or create an incredible amount of work for someone to correct.

Think about these two issues of what you say and what you do. Intentional or not, you have a direct effect and impact on other people every day—that is a huge responsibility. Your presence or inclusion in a gathering should not be taken lightly. Why? Because it's not just about you. It's not about your feelings, your time, your actions, or your thoughts. It can directly relate to someone else's feelings, time, actions, or thoughts.

Remember that what you do says everything about you. I want to share a few unselfish thoughts to live by—call them "Rules for Living."

- If you move it, put it back.
- If you make a mess, clean it up.
- If you borrow it, return it.
- If you value it, take care of it.
- If you can't fix it, call someone who can.
- If you break it, admit it.
- If you unlock it, lock it up.
- If you turn it on, turn it off.
- If you open it, close it.
- If it ain't broke, don't fix it.
- If you drop it, pick it up.
- If it belongs to someone and you want to use it, get permission.
- If it will tarnish someone's reputation, keep it to yourself.
- If it will brighten someone's day, say it.

- If you don't know how to operate it, leave it alone.
- If it's none of your business, don't ask questions.

These seem pretty common sense, don't they? Then why are so many people not doing them? Good question. I don't think I'm alone when I say these are some of my pet peeves.

Think before you speak or do things, and ask yourself the following:

- Will it hurt someone if I say this?
- Will this cause more work for someone else?
- Is this something I need to know?
- Did I leave this the way I found it?
- Will this impact someone's life?

If your answer is yes to any of these, then don't follow through. It's not worth it. and if you do follow through, it will say everything about you.

> *"I've learned that people will forget what you said, people will forget what you did, but people will never forget how you make them feel."*
> —Maya Angelou

How to Keep a Confidence with Someone

Do you know what a confidence is? Do you *really* know what it is? A confidence is merely a trust or a reliance on someone—a trusting relationship, with the assurance that someone will keep a secret. That's *will* keep a secret, not *might* keep a secret. Can you keep a confidence unconditionally or just when it's convenient for you so you can get information? Do you then announce it to the world?

When you're developing a trusting relationship with someone, or if you're already in a close relationship (friends or partners, intimate or not), it's crucial that you keep a confidence, no matter what. Absolutely nothing will ruin a relationship quicker than someone with a loose tongue. When someone tells you information in confidence, but you break that confidence, there is no going back and no forgiving, no matter how simple or small. The person told you something because he or she trusted you.

So why do people have a hard time keeping a secret?

Those "tell-all" people just want the attention of knowing the "scoop," but they were not trustworthy in the first place.

Were you played or used? Maybe. Sadly, some folks can't help themselves. You may not have known your confidant as well as you thought you did. If this has happened to you, I know exactly how you feel, and it's not very comfortable.

Some of us have trouble understanding those who have the need to talk about others and can't keep a confidence. Personally, I cannot tolerate people who share secrets. I'm not a goody-goody type person, but I do understand what a confidence is.

What you say to me stays with me. I developed that confidential motto and way of living from my upbringing and in the career work that I do as a nurse, which requires confidentiality. For me, it's just a habit—whatever information comes in never goes out. Many people, however, are not like that. If you aren't able to keep information to yourself, then the following "food for thought" may help you to help yourself.

Another category of information is generalized, nonpersonal, non-confidential. For this type of category there are still lines that should not be crossed in good faith. To understand this one should ask themselves if it's true, kind, necessary, beneficial prior to sharing information with anyone else. If the answer to any of these are no, you are asking for trouble if you pass it along to someone else. If you share confidential information with which someone has trusted you, the person eventually will find out, and your relationship may be over.

There are so many other life issues on which to concentrate and give your energy. You don't want to worry about a close confidant having a loose tongue.

Be respectful of others' information, and be proud that they trusted you to share their deepest thoughts with you.

> *Sometimes it's just better to be alone than to be in bad company.*

How's Your Attitude Working for You Today?

I had unexpected visitors once while I was watching the Masters Tournament (the "Super Bowl" of professional golf). I soon realized that as happy as I was to see them on this spur-of-the-moment visit, it was probably not a good idea for them to stop by without calling first.

Oh, I don't mean I didn't want their company, and it had nothing to do with the Masters Tournament. It's that they were both in a bad mood, and that was a little awkward. Ultimately, it turned out fine. They lightened up, we had some great laughs, and it was fun.

My point, though, is this: do you realize how your attitude affects others? "The way you treat people says a lot about who you are. Be careful. Your actions are screaming over your words. Say you're ticked off, you're fussing about something, and you can't let it go. No matter how hard you try to cover it up, your attitude will seep through in your body language and affect others.

Here are a few points to keep in mind:

- Your attitude toward others will determine their attitude toward you.
- Your attitude toward life determines life's attitude toward you.
- Your attitude at the beginning of a task will affect the outcome of the task more than anything else.
- Before you can achieve the kind of life you want, you must think, act, walk, talk, and conduct yourself in the way you ultimately wish to become.
- The higher you go in any organization of value, the better the attitude you'll find.
- Keeping successful, positive thoughts in your mind will make all the difference in the world of your ongoing success.
- If you always make people feel needed, important, and appreciated, they will return that same attitude to you.
- Glow in the attitude of well-being. Don't be embarrassed to share visions, desires, and goals with someone you trust.

- Don't talk about your health, even if it's good. If you must talk about your health, only talk with those who are involved and feel comfortable discussing it.
- Don't broadcast your personal problems. It certainly won't help you, and it will only make others uncomfortable.
- Part of a good attitude is to look for the best in new ideas—car bumper stickers, restaurant menus, books, travel slogans, the innocence of a child's words.
- Make it a point to treat everyone you meet with respect, patience, kindness, and encouragement.
- Treat others as you want to be treated yourself. (The Golden Rule still applies: Do unto others as you would have them do unto you.)

These all sound familiar, don't they? Many of us were raised on these points. By following these points, you will enlighten others, and their bad moods will become positive and grateful. It worked on my unexpected visitors that day. They quickly got over themselves, and we had a great visit. Remember that your attitude *does* affect others on so many levels.

The only disability in life is a bad attitude.

Good or Bad, Your Habits Reflect Who You Are

Did you know that your self-image and habits go together? If you change one, you'll automatically change the other. We create habits because they fit us; they are consistent with our self-images and our personality patterns.

When we consciously and deliberately develop new and better habits, our self-images tend to outgrow the old habits and grow into the new pattern. On the other hand, habits are merely reactions and responses that we have learned to perform automatically without thinking or deciding.

At least 95 percent of our behavior, feelings, and responses is habitual. For example, a pianist does not *decide* which key to strike. A dancer does not *decide* which foot to move. These reactions by the pianist and the dancer are automatic.

Similarly, our attitudes, emotions, and beliefs tend to become habitual. In the past, we "learned" that certain attitudes and ways of feeling and thinking were appropriate to certain situations. Now, we tend to think, feel, and act the same way whenever we encounter what we interpret as the same sort of situation.

Habits, unlike addictions, can be changed, modified, or reversed, simply by making a conscious decision and then practicing a new response or behavior.

The pianist can consciously decide to strike a different key. The dancer can consciously decide to learn a new step. It does, however, require constant, positive, mindful practice until the new behavior pattern is thoroughly learned; then they can become habits.

If you do not like your self-image, you need to change your habits. What you do to make that change is entirely up to you; you were not "born that way." The habits you have were formed from a learned behavior. You can choose to change, to learn something new—something better, something more appealing, something more satisfying—by making a conscious decision to change your habits. And when you do make the conscious decision to change your habits, your self-image will also change.

It will not happen overnight; like the pianist and dancer, it requires constant positive, mindful practice until the new behavior pattern is learned, before it becomes habit. Give it a try, but stick with it. I think you will be surprised by how wonderful you'll feel.

Change you habits to a positive response, and your self-image will become more positive ...

Do You Know What Negativity Does to You?

Feeling at your worst, you start looking around and don't see much hope for yourself. You're about ready to give up, but you think maybe a prayer for a breakthrough will be answered. You have given up on all hope of getting anywhere, much less knowing where to start. Then you feel down, then negative, then stressed.

When I got married, I thought of how wonderful life was going to be. I had been raised in such a positive atmosphere, I was as naïve about negativity as I was about life in such a young age. Being around someone for several years is very different than really knowing someone. For my relationship the comic, teaser, prankster becomes dark, possessive, controlling & demanding. These sides all turned into an aggressive abuser verbally at first but quickly turned into a physical abuser daily. There seemed to be a switch within him from when in public & family presence, he was the comical teaser, fun loving prankster. But when in our personal private time he switched to the dark, angry, controlling, demanding soul who only knew how to be verbally & physically abusive all the time when we were alone.

It all began during the Honeymoon, it was an initial abrupt change in him. I quietly wondered who he was. I saw an angry, short tempered, intensely controlling man I didn't recognize. He had no interest in leaving the Hotel to sightsee, participate in activities or do anything except watch television and ordered me around which I found out when I suggested I would go look at some of the sights myself. I wasn't 'allowed' to go by myself.

He began stalking me everywhere, by showing up at work frequently & just staring at me from down the hall, through the windows or doors. He would following me in his car telling me when asked, to 'make sure I went to where I was going' when I told him I was going to the store. He would not 'allow' me to visit my family, demanding to know where I was at every moment. He would become upset and yelling if his shirts were not ironed properly and hung up in the closet to his liking.

He smashed the windows of my car while I was at work and stole the music tapes I had, informing me later, those tapes his tapes.

I literally went from being a happy go-lucky woman to always looking over my shoulder in fear of seeing my husband standing there, knowing that the physical abuse later would be "my" fault because I didn't tell him every detail he thought I should.

All of these abuses continued which to me seemed like an eternity, until one night the whole world stopped for me.

On my way one from the store one evening, I stopped at my parents house, whom I rarely saw since being married. We had a fun conversation and they talked me into watching an early evening TV movie with them. I later noticed it was about 8:30 and I indicated I better get home, never realizing what was waiting for me when I would get there.

When I walked in the house, being in a good for since having a fun time with my parents, I said hi and apologized as I put down the bags from the store on the kitchen table, for how long it had been but Mom & Dad were talking and then got I became interested in a TV movie ...

He suddenly jumped up, ran over to me and began yelling, calling me names, slapping my face, grabbing my arms, pushing me against the wall & hitting me while continuing to yell. Suddenly I found myself up in the air with the pain in my throat and neck from him. This 6'4 man was holding me, a 5'4 woman up against the door with my feet off the floor, by the neck squeezing away my breath while yelling in my face about being told I was not to go anywhere, not to go to my parent's house, not to do what I wasn't told to do ...

Being suspended in the air and pinned to the door, I felt helpless and I could only think 'this is it, I can't get away from him this time". But from out of no where I couldn't hear his yelling or feel the pain in my neck. I just saw the rage and hatred in his face this time as the end, although I wasn't ready for the end, my end this time. I believe I just snapped ...

I quickly broke free, grabbed this tall man, picked him up and threw him across the room, turned toward the door immediately fumbling with the locks on the door, and hearing broken glass behind me. I got the door opened and was on the porch steps when I heard him say:

"look what you did, look at what you did, what until I tell my Mom what you did" ...

When you start changing your thoughts, you'll fuel your movements and choice—you are choosing to do this. First, negative thoughts drain your ambition. Negative thoughts convince you that you're doomed. Negative thoughts expect no hope for you. It's a movement of choice; you are choosing which direction you're going.

Is that what you want? Are you that convinced you're not going to make it? That downward spiral is a conscious choice.

Negative thoughts, feelings, and actions take a lot of work. You spend a lot of time convincing yourself you can't do it. You believe everyone hates you. You give up on any opportunity that comes along to help you. It's a lot of work and stress being negative all the time.

If I had done that—had given up and had been negative about everything—I would have never gotten to where I am now.

Negativity is exhausting—both to you and to those around you. Think about what your body goes through. Feeding your mind negative thoughts, feelings, and actions depresses the neurotransmitters of your brain. The neurotransmitters release the "happy" or "unhappy" substances in your brain, depending on your feelings and thoughts.

But your negativity doesn't stop there. It also affects your primary organs: heart, blood circulating system, liver, pancreas, kidneys, stomach, and intestines. That's pretty much all the primary organs. Negativity stresses the organs, forcing them to work harder.

But wait—that's still not all negativity affects. Your hair thins, becomes more brittle, and falls out. Your nails become brittle and break easily. Your hearing becomes less sensitive. Your internal fluid levels decrease; bowel and bladder changes are significant. Your teeth and oral status deteriorates. Your optic nerves fog, and your pupils become dull. Your skin becomes drier, flaky, and dull.

The effects of constant negativity and the effects of stress on your body are quite similar. Both have significant effects, psychological and physical, on your body that do not result in good outcomes. It's not okay to be negative, down, and stressed all the time. If you are, you affect those around you and break down your body. As a medical professional, I have seen the results in people, and it's not pretty.

So what can you do? Start by being aware of your thoughts and your words. Start be believing in yourself. Start taking action to be positive, even when you don't feel like it.

Choose to be positive, and feed yourself with up lifting thoughts and tasks.Start, believe, choose, have hope, and get up with positive, productive feelings and actions. No one can do this for you. Your negative thoughts and stresses are not only pulling you further down, but they're killing you.

Can you fix it and reverse it? Yes, but you must commit to yourself and stick to it.

By my sudden face with severe fear for my life with my husband's hand around my throat, holding me with my feet off the floor and his body pinning me up against the door all the while he was punching me with his other hand, I snapped, my adrenaline – the fight or flight mechanism in my brain, kicked in and gave me incredible strength that I never had. You have no doubt heard of people having the ability to lift up a car or incredibly heavy object off of someone during a near fatal crisis, that is the adrenaline – fight or flight mechanism in the brain that emergently secretes the epinephrine within you giving you strength you never knew possible.

When I got myself free of his grip from off the floor, picked him up and threw him across the room, I didn't realize at the time, he landed on the wooden glass top coffee table, the legs snapped off and all the contents and glass on the table top shattered and scattered everywhere in the living room. That was all adrenaline, and the words he spoke: "look what you did, look at what you did, what until I tell my Mom what you did" … I experienced an immediate pause and realization that none of this verbal and physical abuse, anger, controlling, demanding, yelling was not my fault as he told it was day after day after day … it was something deep seeded within himself that had nothing to do with me, and those deep issues had begun long before I ever knew him.

Recognize the negative, make a choice and take action to get the negative away from yourself. Remember, no one can do this for, it must be done by you.

Being negative and being stressed is a choice. Choose wisely—for the sake of your body.

Do You Know How to Bury a Good Idea?

At one of my follow-up surgical appointments, I happened to overhear the conversation behind the desk. The staff members were loud and animated (to be honest, those out in the hallway probably could hear them as well) as they shared their ideas about starting a new method in the clinic. Not everyone agreed with the presented ideas; there were negative comments as well. That made me think about my business training, where I learned there are seven ways to bury a good idea, and that is by saying any one of the following statements:

"It will never work."

"We have never done it that way before."

"We are doing fine without it."

"We can't afford it."

"We're not ready for it."

"It's not our responsibility."

"That's not how we used to do it."

If you are using any of these phrases for your work, project, or home issues, you might as well stop and forget it, because you have already "buried" your good idea.

Do or do not. There is no "try."

How Do You Deal with Anger?

When you're forced to deal with loss, hurt, life changes, or stress, anger can build up inside of you. After the initial shock of grief, loss, and frustration, you merge those feelings into anger over your loss, being hurt, the life-changing events you've had to go through, and the stress that's mounting because you can't keep up. If you don't deal with that anger, it will continue to build and build.

How do you deal with anger? Do you ignore it? Do you just add to it? What are you really doing with it, other than taking it out on others. You may deny you have any anger at all, and that's all right, but if you have experienced even one of the mentioned feelings, you are harboring anger.

Even if you think you're not holding any anger, it's important to know how to deal with anger. I had to nail this down about myself while I was going through my life-changing issues. I had to be honest with myself, and you must do this too. It will make a huge difference for you, emotionally and physically.

The first step in resolving anything is to admit you have the issue. Admit your anger. Be honest with yourself about it. It's really okay; you need to admit it.

Next, evaluate your anger. Honestly ask yourself, "What triggers my anger? When am I most likely to feel anger?"

Choose your perception. Slow yourself down, and put the anger trigger in perspective. Turn the triggering situation into a positive situation.

Calm yourself down. If your anger is getting out of control, lower your voice, sit down, and take a few deep breaths. If you're still not calm, get outdoors and walk it out.

Watch your words and actions. When you're angry, you easily say and do things you'll regret later. Be aware of what comes out of your mouth because you can never take back words said in anger. An "I'm sorry" will never erase those words.

Work out your anger. An angry state produce adrenaline, which must be released. So work out your anger—go on a walk, chop wood, weed a garden, mow the yard.

Talk about your anger. Take responsibility for your feelings. Be direct and honest without blaming or attacking. If you overreacted, admit it. The more you honestly communicate about your anger, the more you can control it.

Commit yourself to resolving your anger as soon as possible. Unresolved anger turns into bitterness, feelings of revenge, or both. The sooner you handle your anger, the better it will be for your mental health. And please, never go to bed angry; life is way too short.

Seek help. Be honest and realistic. If your anger persists or is out of control consistently, get professional help. Talk to a counselor, pastor, or physician, and develop a more intense therapy plan. No, you're not crazy; there are times, though, when an outside professional opinion makes the best sense.

Be smart, be safe, and be honest and realistic about your anger issues. Anger will change your attitude and personality and will damage your body. Don't be ashamed of your anger; get t

If you know you have a "short fuse," then do something about it. Ignoring your anger issues is dangerous, for you and for those around you, both emotionally and physically. A "short fuse" is not an excuse; it's a threat. Seek help.

You must take control of your anger and your feelings
before they take control of you.

What Is Happening in the World—and What Can You Do to Help Turn It Around?

The world we were born into has vastly changed. I find it completely unrecognizable. Who are we now? What changed people's values, morals, and standards? How did we get here?

I've never seen so much rudeness, selfishness, impatience, denial, displaced anger, righteousness, and self-preservation. In disbelief, I've watched the immaturity, the disconnecting, the "unfriending," the lack of learning, the spinning out of control, the lack of awareness, and the despicable behavior.

On the other hand, I've found people who are good, kind, positive, and honest and who expect nothing in return. Fortunately, I have embraced those around me and worldwide who have these qualities. Those with whom I am friends and with whom I associate, connect, and work from around the world are kind, caring givers facilitators, and motivators; they are inspirations. They are understanding and help others find their passions. These people do not blame others, fly off the handle at others, or turn their backs on an individual. They're not in denial; they're not short-tempered or arrogant.

You can help turn the world around by just doing your part.

What You Can Do to Help Turn This Around

Here are my thoughts on what the world needs:
We need people:

- who are unafraid or ashamed to stand for the truth, even when it's unpopular
- who can say no with emphasis, even when the rest of the world says yes
- who do not believe cruelty and hard-headedness are the best qualities for achieving success
- who are true to their friends through good and evil, in adversity as well as prosperity
- who will not say they do something "because everybody else does it"
- whose ambitions are not confined to their selfish desires
- who will make no negative compromises
- who will be as honest in small things as in large things
- who will not lose their individuality in a crowd
- who do not hesitate to take chances
- who are larger than their job titles
- who possess opinions and a will
- who put character above wealth
- whose word is their bond
- who cannot be bought

Are good people still out there? Absolutely; the best of the best is still out there.

No one person can tame this world alone, but nothing is too big if we work together, day by day, one step at a time.

So the next time you hear someone say, "This world is beyond help," step up.

Be the one to step forward, reach out your hand, and help someone— not because you have to but because you want to, from your heart.

Be that person for whom those in need are reaching.

Be a fountain of hope, not a drain.

Stop Being So Selfish! How to Handle Those with "Me" Syndrome

Have you noticed how many people have "Me" syndrome? People have "Me" syndrome when they think everything is always about them. They don't think of you, their other friends, or their families. It's all just about them—their "me."

So how should you handle those people? It seems there's only so much you can do. These people are in the same category as folks who are unable to listen to others. Those who don't know how to listen sometimes have Me syndrome.

"Me" people don't really care what you have to say; they're too busy talking and talking over you. They never listen; they just talk. Their responses to you are often inappropriate because they haven't listened.

So how do you handle Me syndrome and those who never listen? You don't handle them; you let them walk away. You cannot help someone who clearly doesn't want to be helped. Their self-directed behavior will not change unless they accept they have a problem, they want to understand the problem, and they want help for it.

The best course of action is to no longer respond to them and walk away. Move on with your own life.

Chances are, they won't even know you're gone. They're too wrapped up in their own agenda and have no intention of changing. They're too self-centered to recognize anything going around them. Chances are, they are not willing to learn new listening skills. All of your energy and time will just be wasted. Letting go is hard, but there are others around you—and even those you don't know yet—who are waiting to find someone just like you. There are those who do listen, care, and are giving to others.

Never chase after someone with Me syndrome. Me syndrome is not normal—listening skills and open-mindedness are not options for them—but here are a few politically correct ways to deal with a Me syndrome individual:

Let the person go. He or she may not come back, but you need to think what you want. If you've spent a lot of energy on the person already but he or she still has a deaf ear, it's truly not worth your time and energy anymore. You cannot change someone who doesn't want to be changed.

Should you let Me syndrome people back into your life? I didn't. They broke my respect, trust, and admiration. Their own credibility was gone for me. Remember that they don't care about you; they care about themselves. Frankly, I can't and won't compete with that attitude.

Those who eventually did try to contact me again got no response. After I let them know where I stood, I didn't see any reason to go backward. Once you've made that decision, you must move on and use your energy forward. And don't feel guilty about walking away. The reality is that Me syndrome people generally don't care that you've moved on; it will be of little interest to them.

Remember, you cannot move forward when you're looking behind you. Life is too short to waste your time on people who don't care. You shouldn't have to "train and teach" people the skills they should have learned while growing up. You deserve respect, kindness, trust, honesty and attention from those around you. You cannot count on any of that from a Me syndrome person.

You have so much to give, and those who receive the "gift of you" should respect you for it.

I am learning how to walk away from people and situations that threaten my peace of mind, self-respect, or my self-worth.

How to Know What You Can Control

We live in a world where everyone wants to be in control. Some people want to control the money, some want to control their businesses, some want to control others.

Remember that being in control is either a healthy way, or an unhealthy way to live. Healthy control is anything that involves only you—your own actions and your own surroundings. Unhealthy control is manipulating others, trying to best others so you can control them, and involving others only for self-gain.

I want to remind you that no matter who you are, what you do, where you live, or how much money you have, there are things that you cannot control.

- You cannot control the length of your life, but you can control the reach and quality of it.
- You cannot control who or what you are, but you can control how you express yourself.
- You cannot control another person's annoying habits, but you can control your own.
- You cannot control the distance your head is above ground, but you can control the quality of the contents you feed into it.
- You cannot control the weather, regardless of what you think, but you can control your reaction to it and plan accordingly.

It's so important to realize you can only control yourself, what you feed into your mind, how you express yourself, and how you treat others. Stop trying to change others; don't waste energy on something you cannot change. Instead, become the person you want to be, the person you were meant to be. Channel your personal energy to something you *can* influence and control—you.

When you see a large group of people, it's fun to hear their various conversations—things that happened, the adventures they had, the people they met. Hearing about others' recent activities and listening to them freely sharing got me to thinking about people in general. More specifically, it made me think about the various types of people with whom we all come into contact and how different we all are.

When I used to watch the news, my thoughts would wander as I considered where the world had gone with regard to the way some people treat others==at least those people who seem to end up on the news. Still, I knew there are wonderful people in this world because I'm blessed to know many of them. The people with whom I associate are from around the globe and are some of the very best individuals you'd ever meet. I feel very lucky and truly blessed to have these people in my life.

To everyone who is in my life—family, friends, business friends and associates with whom I work and interact every day from all over the world—thank you for being in my life. You're all amazing, and I am a better person for having known you.

You never know when you're going to meet someone
who will change your life ... completely.

How to Make Better Choices for Yourself

Do you ask yourself how to make better choices when you wake up every day? Probably not. Most of us have more mundane questions when we wake up—if we have any questions for ourselves at all.

When you get up, however, and begin your daily habits—those things you do without even thinking about them, such as bathroom time, eating, getting dressed—there is something else you should automatically do: make choices.

Take the time to make better choices.

If you create better habits in your daily routine, you won't have to think about how to make better choices for yourself; you automatically will do it every day.

Here are some examples of the choices you can make, which will lead to better choices for yourself.

Choose to:

- love, rather than hate
- forgive, rather than hold a grudge
- smile, rather than frown
- act, rather than delay
- build, rather than destroy
- give, rather than take
- persevere, rather than quit
- praise, rather than gossip
- heal, rather than wound
- pray, rather than despair

I challenge you to pick one you normally don't do on a daily basis—just one—and try it today, then tomorrow, and then every day for a week. If you do this on a regular basis, your choice will be automatic.

Making better choices for yourself every day and consistently following through with them will become daily habits—they'll be automatic. This expression of kindness you do automatically every day is how to make better choices for yourself.

Busy is a choice, stress is a choice, being negative is a choice, and joy is a choice.

How Well Do You Know Yourself?

You have to know yourself in order to function well in life, to succeed, to grow, to love, to flourish, to thrive.

But how well do you really know yourself? Do you know what you're made of and how you think? Do you know your likes and dislikes? If you don't, how will you ever know what your dreams and passions? Simply put, you won't.

Those around you already know how you project yourself; even your pets know.

To really know yourself, think about what you want most in life. Also consider what you think about the most, how you spend your money (and on what), and how you spend your leisure time. With whom do you enjoy spending time? Who or what do you admire? What do you laugh at, or who makes you laugh?

These are the basics of you—your likes, thoughts, desires, enjoyment, and personal finances. If you don't know all of these answers, you need to dig deeper inside yourself to find out. In order to love yourself, which is what you have to do before you can love anyone else, you first need to know about yourself. Only then will the rest follow, your second step: believe in yourself. Once you believe in yourself, you can do anything.

You will never become who you want to be if you keep blaming everyone else for who you are now.

How Do You Come Across When Speaking to Others?

I listen a lot. I hear what people say, how they're saying it, and how they're trying to get their point across. By listening to others, I also learn a lot about them. Of course, this is what we're supposes to do, isn't it? We should listen to others.

I have to admit, though, that when I listen, I'm really listening to their "hidden messages"—those words that are not spoken.

Let me give you an example. I was having a conversation with some folks I hadn't seen in a while—not since before my accident. While they were talking to me—and I really did listen to what was being said—I picked up their unspoken messages. I'll call these *destructive mistakes* that occur while having a conversation:

- Refusing to set aside your own trivial preferences
- Insisting that something is "impossible" just because you can't accomplish it yourself
- Having the delusion that personal gain is made by crushing and destroying others
- Having the tendency to worry about things that can't be changed or corrected
- Neglecting self-development and refinement of the mind and not acquiring the habit of reading to learn new things
- Attempting to compel others to believe and live only as you do

Maybe I'm overly critical about how someone comes across, but the points above are signs of a lack of personal growth.

Listen to yourself and honestly evaluate if you have any of these tendencies when you are trying to get your point across in a conversation. If you have been guilty of any of these, you're not alone—but try to find a way to resolve those points. Be open about new ways, new information, and new growth for yourself. Be aware of the areas where you're lacking and need personal growth. Find a way to overcome your personal weaknesses, and *think* before you insist on getting your own point across.

Enjoy your conversations, but be aware of how others may perceive you without your knowing it. Always be open to learning new things

Channel your personal thoughts and energy to things you can influence and control.

Again, How Well Do You Know Yourself?

When I ask people how well they know themselves, I generally get a few typical answers. Some say they know what they like, how happy or sad they feel, whether they're tired or full of energy, and when they're hungry.

But the question was, I remind them, "How well do you know yourself?" That means how well do you know what you're made of; what makes you the person you really are? What are your innermost thoughts?

Only you know the answers to these questions, and generally, people hold the answers very close to their hearts.

How well do *you* know yourself?

- What do you want the most?
- What do you think about most of the time?
- How do you spend your money and your time?
- Whose company do you enjoy the most?
- Whom do you admire?
- What do you admire?
- What and who makes you laugh?
- What are your dreams?
- In one word, what is your vision?
- What makes you happy?

Were you able to answer the questions? Be honest—how well do you really know yourself?

> *Nothing in life has any meaning except the meaning we give it.*

CHAPTER 3

Stress

Everyone experiences some level of stress every day. Are you aware of how stress affects your body? Stress drains your body to the point where your health is compromised; it can even impact your immune system. In this chapter, you'll find ways to deal with stress and get it under control. You can control stress if you want to, but the key is to work at it consistently.

How to Let Nostalgia Work for You

Do you enjoy thinking about pleasant times you've had, or do you not think back on any past experiences?

We each have our own way of storing memories, both good and bad. Some of us don't want to go back to those memories, even the good ones. We may feel those times are over, and we can't go back, or we may say, "It's just a waste of time to dwell on those times. They aren't real anymore."

Sometimes, however, going back to those nostalgic thoughts can help to ground you, especially when you start going in circles when your life is busy, and you become more and more uptight. Traveling your daily routine at such a fast speed only causes you to lose touch with the everyday little things that touched your heart before you became so busy with filling your head with everyday information. When you purposefully let yourself go back and think about the little things that made your heart smile, it causes an actual physical response in your body that calms you.

It's temporary, sure, but if you do it often enough, it can be more calming than any medication—and there are no side effects. If your deadlines and other work is making you more and more uptight, and you have no outlets to rid yourself of stress, see if you can relate to the following suggestions and memories that will help you to feel happy again:

- The smell and sounds of a warm fireplace
- Climbing to the top of a windy hill with an amazing view
- Looking over childhood photos in the family album
- Watching your now-grown "child" leave home
- Taking a barefoot walk along a sandy beach
- Listening to a rippling brook running over rocks
- Watching your puppy learn how to walk and run while still clumsy
- Seeing an old letter, signed by one who loved you
- Singing your favorite song in the car with your best friend
- Visiting the quiet place where you were raised
- Walking through the woods in the autumn, hearing the crackling leaves beneath your feet, and feeling the chill in the air
- Standing silently beside the grave of a close friend or relative
- Being alone and reading aloud
- Snow, toboggans, ice skating, and sleds
- Graduation diplomas or degrees
- Weddings you were in or attended
- Learning new poems or new song lyrics and melodies
- Christmas Eve, late at night, when everyone else had gone to bed

If you let yourself think back, hear the sounds, smell the scents, and daydream in the memories, things can and will bring a calmness over you.

Saying good-bye to someone you have cared about, these memories can take you to a place that may have brought you so much joy and happiness.

Remember that pleasant thoughts and memories can physiologically bring a calmness to you. Just telling yourself to "calm down" will not help, but nostalgia will.

If you think you have nothing to be nostalgic about, then let your imagination soar. Just be sure you put in the sounds, scents, and visual effects to help it feel more realistic. Where will your imagination take you? Just open your mind and heart, let your imagination take you somewhere more pleasant, almost like a mini-vacation.

"Change your thoughts, and you change your world."-
Norman Vincent Peale

How You Can Break Out of Your Old Habits with New Ones

Are you feeling blah or down, with nothing inside to give? Is your tank empty or even just plain yucky? If so, you are not alone; in fact, you're actually in the majority.

You don't know why you feel like this, but man, it's an awful feeling. Sometimes you just want to crawl up in a ball. These yucky feelings have been building up inside of you for some time. Now that your own inner space is getting full of all those bad feelings, it's coming out in another way. Since your feelings and energy level have been getting lower, you've started to develop low-energy habits.

These habits, however, are not the good kind; they are negative habits.

This habit of feeling blah or having negative thoughts and feelings about hurtful or uncomfortable places are replayed, over and over, like a broken record in your mind. The weight of those negative habits severely weighs you down, like boulders on your shoulders, day and night.

Realize too that negative energy is contagious. When you continue the habits of your down-in-the-dumps, doom-and-gloom outlook, no one will want to be around you. Who wants to be around someone who is always negative? It's incredibly draining; it's exhausting and taxing. You'll find that *you* won't want to be around you either.

Your blah feelings have now progressed into a negative habit. Don't think this habit is unchangeable. This must be resolved immediately. How do you do it? No one else can fix this for you. Only you can do it—and you will—but only if you want to change. There's no pill that will "cure" this negativity. Medications are a temporary mend that cover up the underlying problem, so *just do it.*

How you can break your old habits and create new ones?

- Speak kindly to a stranger.
- Make or bake something for someone—anonymously.
- Keep a promise.
- Do something to give joy to a child.

- Express appreciation.
- Be gentle and patient with an angry person.
- Forgive an enemy.
- Give someone you know a big hug while whispering you love him or her.
- Find a forgotten friend.
- Mend a quarrel.
- Be a listener to someone else's sorrow.
- Give encouragement to an older person.
- Give a soft answer, even though you feel strongly.
- Pray for someone who helped you when you were hurting.
- Turn off the television and just talk.
- Apologize if you were wrong.
- Let up on your demands on others.
- Pet a dog or cat.
- Talk and walk with a friend.
- Smile, laugh a little, and laugh even more.

The habits you have formed *can* be changed. I can assure you, however, that if you choose *not* to change your old negative habits, you will continue to spiral downward and out of control. Start being proactive about yourself, and stop blaming others for where you are at this moment. Be someone you're proud of being and someone others like being around.

> *Turn your cant's into cans and your dreams into plans.*

How to Control Being Overwhelmed

Do you feel you are drowning or out of control, to the point that you can't think, you feel smothered, and you want to just scream?

My friend, I promise you, you're not alone. I have been there myself, and it's terrifying, isn't it? You feel like the walls and the world is closing in, and you can't even breathe. Overwhelming anxiety crept in after my accident. I was unable to do anything. I couldn't, get up or move. I was overwhelmed and terrified. What did I do about it? What can *you* do about it?

First, just *stop!* When you are in over your head, filled with anxiety, fear, worry, shame, or other feelings, you must stop and be still. Give your mind a break, calm yourself, and tell yourself that you *can* do this—because you can. I've been in your shoes, so I know it's possible. You must take things a minute, an hour, and a day at a time. This is about all you can contend with right now, so start there. The last thing you want to do is to think about the pile of whatever you think is important right now. You're not ready yet, so put it out of sight.

You must work up to handling one day at a time. You'll eventually get beyond a day, but start with that. So how do you control being so overwhelmed? One day at a time.

Every day, say the following statements out loud:
On this day,

- I will accept myself and live to the best of my ability.
- I will try to be happy. My happiness is a direct result of my being at peace with myself, and I know what others do or think will not deter my happiness.
- I will say what I mean and mean what I say, with only positive words of encouragement to myself.
- I will not tackle all my problems at once but live moment to moment to my very best ability.
- I will live my life being assertive, not aggressive; humble, not proud; confident to be exactly who I am.

- I will take care of my physical health. I will exercise my mind, my body, and my spirit.
- I will be kind to those around me. I will be agreeable, finding no fault with others. I will not try to improve or regulate others.
- I will remind myself that God has a special place in his heart for me and a special purpose for me to fulfill in this world.
- I will believe in my heart that I *can* do this, I *choose* to do this, and I *will* do this!

Why are these words to yourself so important every day? Your mind is in overdrive, so you must take control of your thoughts before you overheat your brain. You must consciously replace your negative thoughts and pour in the positive thoughts every day.

Think of it as your garden; you must weed and feed—kill the weeds (negative) and fertilize (positive) in your mind. At the end of the day, before you go to bed, be proud of yourself for getting through the day without being overwhelmed. The next day, get up and start again until this becomes a daily habit of positive thoughts and strength.

It may take you a couple of weeks, depending on your issues, but you will get there by doing this same daily routine—it worked for me!

Remember, take things one day at a time, stay positive, and believe in yourself—you *can* do it, and you will handle this.

Accept what is, let go of what was, and have faith in what will be.

Do You Have Control of Your Stress?

When challenges, losses, hurt, and struggles build up, they push you down farther and farther, to the point of smothering or overwhelming you. You are so down you can't think straight. You begin avoiding everything and everyone because you simply can't breathe.

Are you aware that *stress* does exactly the same thing to you? Stress puts you through the same mechanisms as loss, hurt, challenges, and struggles. Stress pushes you to the point of feeling smothered and overwhelmed. You can't think straight, you can't sleep, and you start avoiding things you once enjoyed, even people.

Even if you think you aren't stressed, you might want to pay attention because I'm going to offer a few things that might relieve some of that pressure. You can't conquer the world by yourself, and you can't get back up unless you listen to some ideas.

I did the following things to make myself get back up and take control of my life again. If they're not for you, that's fine; then share them with someone who is having trouble. Remember—stress and life-changing events all result in the same problems, and you must get on top of this before there are physical effects from this turmoil.

- Divert your focus. Diversion gives your mind a break from problem solving and carrying the burdens. It's impossible to be consumed with worry when something else is captivating your interest.
- Develop order. Tidy things up around you and toss clutter. You can restore a sense of calm to a room with a thirty-minute "sort and dump."
- Diffuse. Push the pressures out of your body through a twenty-minute aerobic exercise or a thirty-minute walk.
- Debrief. Talk out your tension and down feelings with a safe and trusted friend.
- Diversify. You must change the channels in your brain. Problem solving is more effective when your mind frequently rests, rather than obsessing on the problem continuously.

- Deliberately rest. Schedule several five-minute breaks during your day to let yourself down and slow your mind and body. Do a task that doesn't require thinking—listen to relaxing music, walk, meditate, pray, or do whatever you can do to let your brain unwind.

- Face your unfinished business. Make amends whenever possible. Give forgiveness rather that carrying a grudge.

- Decide to trust. I found one of the best ways to overcome my fears and overwhelming feelings was to choose to trust myself. You must believe in yourself and trust you will find a way back up and out of the issues going on around you.

- Get back to basics. To see clearly through all the blinding stress and sadness around you; sleep at least eight hours per night, eat well-balanced meals (cut back on carbs, as they can weigh down your mind and body), and exercise (either aerobics or walking at least thirty minutes per day, three times per week.

- Disengage. If you're overwhelmed, step away, give yourself some time, and stop trying so hard. You don't have to fix everything today, nor should you.

- Dig in. Avoiding something only heightens your anxiety. Evaluate what can be done, and just do it. Don't let yourself get stuck in the mud by using an "all or nothing" approach. Pace yourself.

Don't be a "type E." You can't be everything to everybody. Being a type E is more damaging than being a type A. You can't be everyone's hero. and you can't resolve everything. That role is only for one person—God—and he does things in his time.

I heard a phrase from a very dear and trusted friend that is so fitting here: *just know*. That aligns beautifully with the idea of trust. Trust and know that whatever you are struggling with, whatever you are stressing over, you will get through this and will get back up.

> *Accept what is, let go of what was, and have faith in what will be.*

Are You Stressed Out?

Do you feel like you're tied up and can't move, can't breathe, and the rope is getting tighter around your neck? Are you tied up and stuck with a massive rope but don't have a clue where it came from?

When we start falling over hurdles, can't deal with challenges, and become overwhelmed, we may feel we've gone lower than hitting rock bottom. Loss—financial loss, relationship loss, or job loss—can pull us down farther and farther every day. Issues build within us, and eventually we have to determine what's causing this downward spiral. Many of these feelings could be caused by stress.

The following are a few danger signs of stress. See if any fit your situation.

You might be under too much stress if you

- don't laugh as much as you used to;
- talk more negatively than usual;
- become forgetful and absentminded;
- find yourself irritable or impatient with things you normally tolerate;
- get distracted easily and have trouble concentrating;
- have difficulty getting to sleep and feel exhausted when you wake up;
- suffer from frequent headaches or stomach pains and nausea;
- sense that you are just one step away from falling apart;
- use alcohol, drugs, or food to help you relax;
- change your priorities, postponing what is important to accomplish what is not important; or
- offer a lame excuse for canceling a get-together with friends and then just sit at home by yourself.

If any of these sound familiar, you likely are in over your head, and your mind and body are already reacting. Take an honest look inside yourself to determine what is causing your stress, and then act to eliminate it. The signs of stress need to be addressed, and you are the only one who can resolve the issue. That doesn't mean, however, that you shouldn't ask for help. Ask your spouse, partner, friend, family member, or anyone else with whom you have an unconditional relationship and good communication to work with you to help you spot and resolve your stress. An objective observer can add a fresh perspective and see things that you might not recognize.

If your stress is caused by a relationship and you can't work it out, then get out and walk away. If your stress is due to a long physical recovery after an injury or illness, make your rehabilitation and therapy your daily chore to get stronger faster. If it's your job and you can't resolve job issues, find another job with less stress. If it's stress over money, construct a budget to get yourself on track. Regardless of your education or income level, you do not have to go through life so stressed, especially from a job.

Stress will not just disappear, and your physical and emotional health will only get worse until your issues are resolved. This must be your priority—to make yourself stress-free. When you do, your life will feel so much lighter and happier. Find a way to get rid of your stress before your stress changes your life.

Busy is a choice, stress is a choice, and joy is a choice.

How to Take Time for Yourself and Recharge

"I can't just 'chill.' I have too much to do!"

Have you ever made this statement? If you have, then that's a problem. Not taking time for yourself is unhealthy and, frankly, selfish. When you spend all your time running around, jumping from task to task, all you're doing is stressing yourself out.

Remember that stress builds up and is bad for your health. Everyone needs time to "chill out" and recharge. Well, more to the point, your body needs time to chill out and recharge. Your brain also needs time to recharge—to declutter, get the noise out, and empty out the distractions.

Here are some thoughts on how you can chill out and get yourself recharged again:

- Take a drive and find a chill-out spot where people don't know you. You might discover a favorite coffee hangout, a lake, café, or state park. Each time you arrive at that special destination, you'll know it's your special place to just sit and read, or dream, or enjoy the quietness that's not available at home.
- Spend the afternoon at a large bookstore. Find an overstuffed chair, sip a cup of coffee or tea, read an interesting book that caught your eye, take a nap, or even pray quietly. Notice the scent of the bookstore—the aroma of published books.
- Develop a new hobby or revisit an old hobby. If you don't know what to choose, do an online search for hobbies. Carve out an hour a day, minimum, to let yourself get involved in the tasks of the hobby and enjoy the feeling of accomplishing the tasks—it's good for the soul.
- Schedule a weekly round of golf, tennis, racquetball, basketball, or other sport for a regular chill-out time away from home.
- Go bowling or even join a league. There's something very therapeutic about picking up a solid ball and throwing it at ten pins.
- Take up gardening. Some people don't have the patience for gardening, but you might discover how relaxing it can be to dig in the dirt and grow flowers or vegetables and fruits.

- Take an aerobics or martial arts class that focuses more on stretching or exercise than on fancy fighting moves.
- Take music lessons on an instrument you've always wanted to learn how to play.

These chill-out ideas should get you started and may trigger other ideas for activities you never considered taking the time to do. If you don't take time for yourself, your life will pass by, and you will not be a participant but a spectator.

Your daily life consists of the sights, smells, feelings, sounds, and calmness that comes over you when you just let yourself be you— without guilt. Don't wait until you retire to work on you; that day may never come, or you may forget what it was that you always wanted to do.

Every day has meaning, every moment has a lesson, and every second has an option. If you don't slow down and seize those now, your life will have meant nothing. Twenty years from now, you will be more disappointed by the things that you didn't do than by the things you did do.

Everyday, is a second chance …

How to Understand the Signs of Burnout

Have you ever heard the following comments from a coworker or friend? Maybe you've made similar comments yourself:

- "I just can't concentrate. What's wrong with me!" You have done that same task a hundred times, and you can't seem to get it together.
- "I just feel so blah. Am I sick?" You used to do twice as much work as you currently are doing, but now you can't keep up and wonder if something is physically wrong.
- "I don't want to go out with my friends today. I'd rather be alone." You are not eating or sleeping the way you use to do, and you don't feel like socializing. Are you ill?

These are just some of the signs of burnout. The term "burnout" often is used quite loosely. People may say they're "burned out" when they might have signs of something more serious. Conversely, some people have the symptoms of burnout but think they are coming down with an illness. Keep in mind that the symptoms of burnout vary from person to person and may not be typical in everyone. In addition, extreme symptoms of burnout should be discussed with your physician. The following, however, are typical signs of burnout:

- lowered productivity
- avoiding people
- poor concentration
- hard to get motivated
- loss of enjoyment
- change in appetite
- lack of energy
- difficulty making decisions
- lack of emotion
- lack of interest
- trouble sleeping

If you experience additional signs that you think might indicate burnout, consult your physician. If not identified correctly, burnout can have long-term effects on your health and mental state. Early detection and identification is very important.

There's no magic pill to correct burnout, but there are things you can do about it before it gets out of control. See your physician for your long-term health and well-being. You only have one life and one body; if you ignore the symptoms of burnout, then you are neglecting yourself. Be aware of any changes going on with you and your body. If you think something's "off," then talk to someone about it.

Sometimes, it's ok if the only thing you do today, is breathe …

How to Gain Back Control of Your Life

"I have so much going on I can't breathe!"

Who doesn't know someone like this? Maybe it's you. Work, kids, school, deadlines, cleaning, laundry, house maintenance, bills, day care, appointments, pet care, dinner, traffic—the list goes on.

Breathe. Seriously, *breathe.*

You already know you're moving at a dead run all the time. You may already have reached the point where the overwhelming effects are hitting you.

So, what do you do?

First, do *not* panic. It's easier than you might think. For you to juggle all you have going on; you must find a way to balance yourself. There are many things you could do, but let's focus on only five things right now:

1. Pay attention to yourself. If you don't stay healthy, you'll be less able to handle the stress of work and home—and that leads to burnout.

2. Stop procrastinating. It takes much more energy to fret over not doing a project than actually doing it. Save your energy for better things, and just get started.

3. Simplify. If the housecleaning is weighing you down, get a house cleaner once a week, or twice a month, or monthly. If you're doing too much, say no to things that you don't want to do or don't have time to do.

4. Be a kid again and play. Give your family or friends one-to-one time. Have a long talk over coffee or tea. Watch TV with yours kids or get down on the floor and play with them. Have fun and share a good laugh—it's good for you.

5. Be grateful. Although you may be in the most hectic time in your life, there still are things for which you can be thankful. Reflecting on the good things in your life helps keep an important balance in your outlook.

You might have noticed each of those are about *you*. These points refer to the most important factor in all that's going on—*you*. For you to be able to sustain a healthy lifestyle and enjoy your life with others, you must look inward. If you don't take care of yourself, you will not be there for anyone else.

"I have found that if you love life, life will love you back."

—Arthur Rubinstein.

How to Fit Exercise into Your Day without Going to a Gym

"I do not have time to exercise," you might say.

Okay, I hear you. You don't have time—or money or desire—to exercise. I get it. I hear comments all the time from patients and others, such as, "Don't tell me to go join a gym. I can't afford it," or "I don't have time for exercising in a gym."

Well, good news—you don't have to join a gym or a class, shell out any money, or even think about an organized way of exercising. You can do it on your own. I have been advising patients and those around me for years about another way of exercising. In fact, you might already be doing some of these "exercises" without realized it.

Here's how to exercise on your own:

- When you go to the mall, park your car at the farthest end of the parking lot, and walk vigorously to the door. Walk completely around the mall before you start shopping. Walk directly to the back of a store and shop moving toward the front of that store.

- Take an exercise break instead of a coffee break. Keep a pair of tennis shoes at your workplace and walk around the block a couple of times. If you can't go outside, walk up and down the stairs of the building during your break.

- If it's practical, ride your bike to work instead of driving or taking other transportation. If this is not practical, ride your bike or walk on errands or when going to the grocery store.

- If you take the bus, train, or subway to work or school, don't board it at the closest stop to your home. Instead, walk to a stop that's twenty or thirty minutes away.

- Use the stairs instead of the elevator. Set a rule for yourself that any time you are going up or down fewer than five floors, you take the stairs.

- Set your alarm fifteen minutes early each day, and take a short, brisk walk. This is the best way to get your circulation going and wake you up first thing in the morning.

- If you cannot find thirty to fifty minutes a day for regular exercise every day, do the next best thing. Find five or six five-minute internals throughout the day to get up and move around.
- During or just after your lunchtime, go outside or to a mall and walk briskly for thirty minutes. Even if this is the only time you can carve out of a day, you'll have done your "workout" for the entire day.
- When you're watching TV, ride an exercise bike, walk on a treadmill, or use other equipment. If you don't have exercise equipment, jump rope or do ten sit-ups during every commercial break. Build yourself up to twenty sit-ups, then thirty, and finally fifty.
- If you can't fit any exercise into your workday, do it right after work. When you get home, make yourself walk around the neighborhood for thirty minutes. This also is a great way to empty your mind of any stress from the day and clear your thoughts—and to get landscaping ideas from your neighbor's yards.

Everyone can do at least three of these suggestions. Remember the importance of your health and exercise. If you spend your days working on a computer, the suggestions are particularly important to do every day.

I want to mention one last thing about exercise: it's the only way to rebuild and maintain your strength, stamina, and health. If you don't exercise every day, you lose strength, muscle tone, and respiratory and circulatory stamina. Your body doesn't ask for anything, but the best thing you can do for your own good health is to exercise.

Since my accident, I have worked up to incorporating every one of the exercise suggestions into my own home therapy program (although I'm still working on the five flights of stairs).

Remember, you are the only one who can change your habits. Start changing this one today.

The Benefits of Moving Around

It's a simple fact: exercise is good for you.

For many of us, the first thing we think about when told we need to exercise is how much it might cost to join a gym, sports center, or athletic club. We also might feel deflated by the thought of going to go to a establishment to work out in front of people you don't know. You may be a little uncoordinated and spend your time focusing on how uncomfortable you are and how much you'd rather be anywhere else.

Getting out of your comfort zone, however, is a good thing. Your mind becomes alert when you attempt new things, meet new people, and do something good for your body (which probably needs a little attention, by the way).

Maybe you'd rather think of exercise in another way; think of it as "moving around." I want to tell you what a little moving around does for your body and your mind. Here are the benefits:

- improved sense of well-being
- more energy
- less stress
- improved quality of sleep
- improved ability to cope with stress
- increased mental acuity
- increased stamina
- increased productivity
- increased physical capabilities
- fewer injuries
- improved immunity to minor illnesses
- improved overall health
- increased efficiency of heart and lungs
- reduced cholesterol levels
- increased muscle strength
- reduced blood pressure
- reduced risk of major illnesses such as diabetes and heart disease
- weight loss

- improved appearance
- improved posture
- toned muscles
- enhanced social life
- improved self-image
- increased opportunities to make new friends
- increased opportunities to share an activity with friends or family

Do you have to go to a gym or club to do this? As I've mentioned, no, you don't. In addition to the earlier suggestions, you can "move around" in parks, hiking areas, or even your home. Shut off the TV and computers, and work around the house. Walk up and down your stairs carrying one thing at a time. Instead of letting your dog out into the yard, put him on a leash and take him for a walk. Walk to get a paper, walk to the post office, or walk around the block. Find creative ways to use your feet, not your wheels. You'll be healthier and sharper and will feel a lot better.

As I increase my activity, I am healing my mind and every one of my organs by releasing stress from my body.

CHAPTER 4

Relationships

I am not an expert on relationships, but I do know that healthy relationships are related to your attitude, mind-set, health, belief, patience, and forgiveness. A relationships is much more than just two individuals who love each other. A relationship involves an association with another individual or group. For this association to work, you must look at yourself and what you are contributing to that relationship. See if any of the following ideas surprise you or f they help you look at the other side of your association.

How to Determine Whether It's Like or Love

Before I get into this topic and offer suggestions on how you're supposed to *know* if it's love, I must share a disclaimer of sorts—I am not a formally trained relationship expert or marriage counselor. As I've mentioned, I'm a registered nurse, which doesn't make me an expert on this topic, but I have additional formal training as a counselor, which at least allows me to be "politically correct" in sharing a few thoughts. Keep in mind, though, that each individual circumstance is different, so my suggestions are not meant as a cure-all.

With that said, let's talk about *like* and *love*.

Having a relationship of any kind starts with an attraction to another person's looks, career, stance on a topic, and so on. Regardless of what caused that attraction, it made you notice and listen to that individual.

Eventually, that initial attraction becomes admiration because of how the person got to you and hit your mind and heart in a way that enabled you to relate to his or her words. This admiration progressed to your looking forward to more information from that individual to learn more. If the person is on social media, you likely decided to "follow" him or her.

From here, the admiration progressed to a respect of that individual's knowledge and consistency, and you experienced a feeling of internal "safeness" when you listen to the person or even when you are around him or her.

From this point, your respect may progress to a mutual *like* from possible reciprocated contact or comments you may have shared, and you received replies in return. The mutual like between you may remain just that—someone you like, respect, admire, and who piqued your interest when your paths first crossed.

Liking someone as an acquaintance, friend, or relationship partner has different meanings for different people. Love in a friendship or relationship also has different meanings, based on what type, degree, and stage of the love. The pattern of how you progress is different for everyone and may be very different for you than what I've indicated.

This can be confusing, can't it?

This is why so many people in various situations may have problems—because *like* and *love* have very different meanings, levels, and stages for everyone.

Because there are so many meanings, I will share my thoughts on what love is and is not. Here's how to determine whether it's like or love:

- Love will always believe.
- Love is loyal, no matter what the cost.
- Love is never glad about injustice.
- Love will always defend.
- Love does not hold grudges.
- Love is not irritable or touchy.
- Love does not demand its own way.
- Love will hardly notice when others do it wrong.
- Love will always expect the best.

- Love is never rude.
- Love is never selfish.
- Love is never arrogant.
- Love is never prideful.
- Love is never boastful.
- Love is never envious.
- Love is never jealous.
- Love is kind.
- Love is patient.
- Love is giving.
- Love is respectful.
- Love is passionate.
- Love is never forced.
- Love gives you peace.

Love comes from the heart, not from your mind. The points in the above list will come naturally from your heart. They will *not* be expected, as if on a checklist, from your mind.

Only you know what's going on inside your heart and mind; only you can distinguish between like and love. If you still aren't sure, read the list again, pausing between each point to let it sink in.

How will you know whether it's like or love?

You will "just know."

Love is what you say; love is what you do.

You Can Build a Friendship When Dating

You don't have to be married to build a friendship within a relationship. Relationships are about trust, honesty, two-way communication, listening, and sharing. If you are dating, you have the same opportunities to build a friendship as those who are married—if you both have your priorities right. Marriage and dating are *not* about sex. It's about building a relationship, a friendship with someone.

You can build a friendship while dating. Here's what to keep in mind when you enter the "dating zone":

- Make it a point to understand the other person's viewpoint.
- Listen to the other person's heart, not just his or her words.
- Ask open-ended questions.
- Do activities together that are equally fun.
- Be yourself. Don't put on an act just to make the person to like you.
- Explore new interests and hobbies.
- Keep physical contact to a minimum.
- Talk with an older couple of faith, and discover how they built their friendship.
- Read a good book together and discuss how its content can help you strengthen your relationship.

The more you know about someone before you increase the intensity of your friendship, the fewer negative surprises there will be in the future.

I believe in letting chivalry rule and allowing the man to ask out the woman. I feel that traditional path speaks volumes about a woman's morals, and she won't appear desperate, impatient, and controlling. Never forfeit your morals and beliefs for a moment in a hormonal surge. You will never be able to erase what you've done and the impression you've made.

Have patience with all things but first of all with yourself.

How You Can Make Someone in Your Life Feel Special

In gatherings of family and friends, there often is a familiar discussion among women, with comments such as "It's just not the same anymore! He just doesn't seem to pay attention or treat me like he used to."

We all have our preferences of how we want to be treated, how our time together should be spent, and how our relationship is going. Whether you are married or single or "relationship" refers to a best friend, being special /to anyone is an awareness you must not take lightly.

People get hurt easily and may feel offended at the drop of a hat. "Hormonal" or not, woman *are* different when it comes to their priorities, feelings, needs, and thoughts.

Some men may feel in over their heads with this deep subject, but I have a few thoughts and suggestions for them too. It's not a clinical dos and don'ts list of what to do. Instead, these are my ideas on things men may not have considered. If you find one or more of the following suggestions appealing and are willing to try them, you'll find yourself on the "good list." If you think these suggestions would never work with her, then you're on your own. Here, then, are ways a man can make the woman in his life feel special:

- Ask her input before making decisions.
- Encourage her to take time out with her friends.
- Find a way to save something from every paycheck.
- Call her if you're going to be more than fifteen minutes late.
- Write out a list of all your important documents and where you keep them.
- Shave on your day off.
- Hold her hand when you lead the prayer.
- Make sure you refill the car's gas tank, check the tires, and keep it in good running condition.
- Be sure to keep your home repaired and in good order.

- Be understanding when she forgets to enter a check in the ledger.
- Buy her a rose bush as a surprise (and plant it for her).
- Occasionally eat quiche and dainty desserts with her at a Victorian restaurant.
- Give her a back and shoulder rub with *no* expectation of making love.
- Ask her out on a date and plan the complete date yourself, including making the reservations.
- Have a good conversation, even when you'd rather read the paper or watch TV.
- Hold her warmly when she cries and tell her you're there for her.
- Carefully clean or polish her shoes for special occasions.
- Ask her to dance when you hear that love song you share.
- Remember to carry Kleenex or a clean handkerchief when you go to a romantic movie.
- When she worries about getting older, tell her she will always be beautiful.

A woman's thoughts, priorities, needs, and desires, are so different from a man's. Men, don't jump in over your head.

Don't ever assume

- she knows because she doesn't;
- she doesn't want to talk because she does;
- she's tough and can handle it because she shouldn't have to do so alone;
- she wants to do it herself because she doesn't;
- she can do whatever she wants because she can't;
- she just knows the way you are and accepts it because she may hate it;
- she feels important to you because she might not;
- she loves your unshaven look because she might hate it; or
- she knows you're always late because she doesn't.

Relationships are a two-way street and require communication, respect, sacrifices, compromises, and showing that you care.

Again, men and women think differently, do not have the same priorities, do not have the same types of feelings, and do not have the same thoughts. Men, take the time to be more attentive now before she's worn out from trying to understand you.

A woman is not a man's mother, keeper, or servant. She is his partner, lover, confidant, best friend, and your number-one fan.

However, she can also be his worst enemy.

So, men, proceed with caution, take the hints, try the suggestions (more than once), and understand that women do not think like men. I hope you heed this advice. Whatever you decide to do, God speed!

Never push a loyal person to the point where she or he no longer gives a damn.

"It's Just Not the Same Anymore!"

Now it's time to let the women know how they can make the men in their lives feel special. The following are **myths** about men:

- A man can't think for himself.
- A man has a one-track mind.
- A man doesn't have a sensitive side.
- A man is all about beer and his buddies.
- A man doesn't think before he does something.
- A man thinks the entire house is the clothes hamper.
- Sex is always at the top of his list.
- A man has selective hearing.
- A man will think of you last.
- A man is as messy as a child.

Believe it or not, most of these "facts" are not true; they're myths. Just as with women, men have an entirely different "wiring" process with their thinking, priorities, habits, feelings, and emotions than do women.

Men develop with more learned behaviors than women do. That is not to say, however, men are not adept at learning other ways of thinking, setting priorities, creating habits, or showing feelings and emotions. Deep down, men do want to do the right thing, but they may not be aware of what to do. So let me offer some thoughts to the women on what they can do to make the men in their lives feel special. Women, do the following:

- Ask yourself this question every day: "What's it like to be with me?"
- If you're married, keep the bedroom tastefully decorated and free of clutter, with him in mind.
- Bake homemade cookies for him to take to work.
- Buy him new socks and underwear on ordinary days, not on holidays or as birthday gifts.
- If you have kids, help them be excited about Dad coming home.

- Trade babysitting with friends so you can have a night at home alone with him.
- Try to be home (work schedule permitting) and off the phone when he gets home.
- Try to be up in the morning when he leaves for work, activities, or planned projects.
- Try to go to bed at the same time he does.
- Be understanding if he falls asleep in the recliner or on the couch after a hard workday.
- If he takes a lunch to work or to an activity, pack it for him.
- Watch his favorite TV sporting events with him.
- Admire him for his strength and significance.
- Develop a genuine interest in his work and hobbies.
- When he gets home, give him space to first relax.
- If you're married, be as concerned about your looks as you were when you were dating.
- If you're still dating, you should be concerned about your looks.
- On your day off, comb your hair and wear a little makeup.
- Stick to your budget.
- Compliment him in front of your friends, his and your parents, and the kids.
- Keep his favorite snacks and drinks on hand.
- Do not interrupt or correct him when he's telling a story. It's his story.
- Understand and be supportive when he wants to spend time enjoying sports or hobbies with his friends.
- Keep lovemaking fresh and exciting. Remember he has more frequent desires than you have.
- Randomly write short, sweet notes or draw funny pictures and leave them in his lunch, toolbox, on his desk, in his car, or in his pocket.

These suggestions never get old and always will warm his heart. Do not assume he knows what you are thinking, he does not, so you will need to understand & deal with it.

Women are smart, very perceptive, and experts at multitasking, but they will never understand men, any more than men will ever understand women. It's a scientific fact that men and women use different parts of their brains every moment of every day. My saying that men and women are "wired" differently refers to this fact.

Women cannot change men any more than men can change women.

Let's all just understand that we have different thought processes, accept it, and complement each other's presence.

Women, you are now forewarned about men. What you choose to do with this information and list of suggestions is entirely up to you. God speed.

> *Channel your personal feelings and energy to the thing you can influence and control—you.*

How to Say What's in Your Heart
When You Don't Know How

"You *never* say anything nice to me!" That is a strong statement, isn't it? Sadly, in so many families, it probably is true. Why does this happen? Has it happened in yours? That is something only you can answer. You and you alone, as a person and as a family, have the ability to change what you say and how you say it.

Here are a few examples of what to say when you don't know how to express what's in your heart. By making a habit of using the following words daily, you will make a difference in someone else's life:

- You make my day.
- I'm proud of you.
- You are a joy.
- That's so creative.
- Way to go!
- Magnificent.
- Bingo! You did it.
- I knew you could do it.
- You are such a good helper.
- You are so special to me.
- I trust you.
- What a treasure you are.
- Hooray for you!
- Beautiful work.
- You are a real trouper.
- Well done.
- I support you.
- You're wonderful.
- I'm praying for you.
- I'm so proud; I'm busting my buttons.
- You light up my day.
- I couldn't be prouder of you.
- I have to hand it to you.

- You sure tried so hard.
- You are the best.
- You remembered.
- You're so responsible.
- I love you.
- You figured it out.
- You are such a good listener.
- Give me a big hug.
- You are awesome.
- I appreciate you.

Simple words, aren't they? But you have no idea how meaningful they are to others. When you say these words (or other positive comments) with a big smile and with feeling—*boom!* Share some of these sentiments with your family, friends, and others. and watch their reactions of gratitude.

You will make a difference by sharing something so simple. If you do use any of these kind words, however, they must come from your heart,

Be kind. Everyone you see is fighting a battle you may know nothing about, even within your family.

How Do You Know What Love Really Is?

Most of us think we know what love really is, don't we? Well, we don't. So many have their own ideas, but when it comes right down to it, it's like anything else—their own versions.

I hope that as you read the following words, you will let each phrase soak in slowly. See if any of these have been a part of your life. (If they haven't, they should be.)

How do you know what love really is?

- Love is a flame that warms but never burns.
- Love does not magnify defects.
- Love finds the element of good and builds on it.
- Love delights in giving attention, rather than attracting it.
- Love knows how to disagree without becoming disagreeable.
- Love rejoices at the success of others instead of being envious.
- Love is not about sex. Love is not about being someone's number one. Love is not about being someone's hero.
- Love is about finding the best in others. Love is about being a giver to others. Love is about being proud of others' accomplishments.
- Love is always about making a difference in others' lives.

Falling in love is not a choice; to stay in love is.

How You Can Mend Your Relationship

"Why should I be the one to apologize?" you might say. "Seriously, why is it always me? It's not fair!"

Relationships and friendships are not about being fair. Being close to someone is not about keeping score of who did what, when, at which time, or if it's now his or her turn.

Relationships of any kind are, frankly, much like a marriage (without the sex, of course), because it's about compromise, understanding, communication, trust, honesty, love and caring, support, and admitting when you are wrong.

Why should you be the one to apologize? Because in a relationship, you and your loved one do not keep score on one another; you're both wrong. One of you causes an issue, the other one reacted to it, and you each blamed the other—it's a stalemate. So how can you mend your relationship?

- Locate the trouble spot.

This is called the "diagnosis" step. Step back and try to assess what went wrong. Where did the misunderstanding begin? How did you get into this vicious circle of put-downs and blame?

- Apologize when you're wrong.

All of us are wrong, plenty of times. It's very silly to let pride and insecurity keep us from saying so and patching up the relationship. Norman Vincent Peale wrote often: "A true apology is more than just acknowledgment of a mistake. It's recognition that something you have said or done has damaged a relationship, and that you care enough about the relationship to want it repaired and restored."

Check to see if your emotions are spoiling your relationship. If a large number of your close relationships go sour, you might ask yourself if you emotional patterns of relating to others are causing the problem. Are you using old methods that no longer work to relate to others?

Each of us has emotional needs, and each of us has acquired a bagful of "tricks" along the way for getting those needs met. Unfortunately, we can learn some very neurotic ways of meeting those needs, and those neurotic patterns can get us into trouble again and again.

Do you have an excessive need for approval? The better a person's self-image, the better friend or partner he or she is likely to choose, resulting in a better relationship—and that, in turn, leads to an enhanced self-image. People with poor self-images, however, tend to choose jerks for friends; hence, the relationship is likely to go bad, and their self-images are further lowered because of their failure. The lesson here is obvious: You cannot depend on others for your sense of self-worth. Your self-worth must come from within you.

Relationships are wonderful, but it's a two-way street of give and take. Give someone special in your life a hug today.

Friends are the most important ingredient in the recipe of life.

How Can You Help Someone Who Is Afraid?

Everyone is afraid of something—and that includes people of all ages, not just children. The movie character Indiana Jones was terrified of snakes! I know of incredible weight builders who are scared to death of spiders. Other presumably brave people are afraid of the dark, water, bugs, dogs, horses—the list goes on.

What is feared is not the issue here; it's how we can help individuals with their fears. Remember, age has nothing to do with it. The following suggestions can be used on children, teenagers, and adult women and men. Here's what to do when someone is afraid of something:

- Be close to the person. Just having the presence of someone safe is calming.
- Touch the person. Holding hands, giving hugs, rubbing his or her back, and any form of reassuring affection helps.
- Speak gently and confidently. Your voice is a point of familiarity and safety, so watch your tone. If you're not calm yourself, you'll make it worse for the one who's scared.
- Listen. Let the person tell you about his or her fears. Be accepting, no matter how irrational. Be attentive and patient. Remember, what the person says is very important to him or her.
- Choose your words and actions carefully. Never laugh or make fun of someone who is fearful. This experience is traumatic. You're there to help, not make the person feel worse.
- Give the person something specific to do. Taking action helps the person to feel like he or she has some power when overwhelmed.
- Give a positive focus. When the person thinks of something safe and reassuring, fears don't seem so big.
- Pray with the person. Seeking God's protection or comfort is something we all need. Reminds the person God is always close, and he always cares.

- Give the person something familiar to hold. Familiar objects, like a blanket, photograph, necklace, ring, or stuffed animal, help children relax—adults too.
- Reassure the person that there is always a way out.
- Teach the person how to problem solve and figure out what to do. Come up with as many solutions as possible. Reassure him or her that things that seem very frightening now often don't seem so bad after a time.
- Remind the person that we all have fears.
- Tell the person what frightens you and how you've handled it.
- Remind the person how brave he or she is.
- Remind the person of other incidents he or she has gotten through with his or her strength.
- Being afraid of something is not a sign of weakness. It's simply an object, item, creature or being, about which the person might not have learned to properly overcome his or her fear.

Helping someone get through a fear is a great teachable moment. The best thing you can do for someone who is fearful, besides being there, is helping the person to learn how to face that fear. It may help again the next time that fear comes up.

Fear is merely the lack of understanding about the unknown.

When You Say "I'm Sorry" Too Much

I think we all know people who say "I'm sorry" all the time. Even if you ask them to stop saying it, they keep on saying it! Why in the world do they do that? It might be habit, lack of something to say, overachieving, trying to please you, or feeling inferior to you.

Saying "I'm sorry" is often misused or stated at inappropriate times, but when is the correct time to say it?

Only say "I'm sorry" when you have been:

- wrong
- rude
- defensive
- impatient
- negative
- hurtful
- insensitive
- forgetful
- confused or confusing
- Also say "I'm sorry" when you have:
- neglected, ignored, or overlooked something important to someone you love
- damaged or misused something that is not yours (even if it was an accident
- not said "I'm sorry" as sincerely and quickly as the situation needed

Saying I'm sorry to someone is meant as an apology for doing or saying something in error or that was hurtful. It's not meant to be just something to say. If there's not a genuine reason for being sorry about something, then don't say it.

Why is this such a big deal?

If you repeatedly say "I'm sorry" as a sentence-filler, then when you actually *are* sorry about something, you will not be taken seriously.

> *Replace I'm sorry with thank you; instead of 'sorry I'm late', say 'thank you for waiting on me'. Just change your mindset.*

Are You Able to Forgive and Forget?

Everyone makes mistakes, says or does something wrong, and hurts someone without thinking. You've done that, haven't you? Others likely have done it to you. Sometime in your life, someone has said something hurtful to you that made you step back and say, "Wow." If not, you're lucky because when that happens, the hurt you feel can change a relationship if you don't handle it properly. So what do you do? Wait for an apology? If that person did apologize, would you forgive him or her? What if the person acted as of nothing was wrong?

The ability to "forgive and forget" is really overrated. You may be able to forgive, but that stinger, the hurt or pain, and the changed image you have of that person is something from which you may not recover.

How do you handle a situation like this because you really do care about that person? No one can tell you what to do in your situation, but I can give you basic guidelines that might give you something to work on.

- Be patient. If the hurt is deep, you can't forgive in just a few moments.
- Take the initiative. Don't wait for the other person to apologize.
- If the forgiven person wants to reenter your life, it's fair to demand truthfulness. Help him or her to understand the hurt you've felt. Then you should expect a sincere promise that you won't be hurt that way again.
- Forgive the person, not the incident. It seems almost impossible to forgive someone for being a bad person. However, remember you accepted that person into your life. Instead, focus on the particular act that hurt you.
- Don't expect too much. To forgive doesn't mean you must renew a once-close relationship. That wound is fresh; give it time to heal.
- Discard your self-righteousness. A victim is not a saint. You too will need forgiveness someday.
- Separate anger from hate. To dissolve your hate, face your emotion and accept it as a natural reaction. Then talk about it

with the one who hurt you, if you can do it without escalating the hatred, or with a trusted third party for an outside opinion.

- Forgive yourself. This is the hardest of all. It's critical to be sincere and straightforward. Admit your fault. Relax your struggle to be perfect. Then be concrete and specific about what is bothering you. Your action or reaction may have been evil, but you are not.

Play it by ear for your particular circumstance, but deal with it, address it, and move on.

Remember, communication requires listening too. Your perception of the situation may not have been the intent. Do as much listening as you do talking when facing the other person.

You may never forget what occurred, but you have to forgive in order to move forward.

Life is 10 percent of what happens to you, and 90 percent of how you react to it.

Are You Fighting All the Time,
Even with Yourself?

Does there always seem to be something or someone that pushes your button? Do you find that whenever you try to do something, somehow it goes wrong? Why is it when you're late traffic is always in your way? You're probably exhausted all the time too, aren't you?

Stop giving so much power to other people and things! You're letting "things" drain you; you gave up before you started. You are the one who controls your "buttons" and who can push them. You are the one who controls your task of how things go when you are doing them. You are the one who controls how late you are (the traffic is not the problem). You are the one who controls how much energy other people and things drain from you.

Are you fighting all the time, even with yourself?

If you're going to fight, you need to fight about things that mean something to you, not the petty little things. If you want to fight, here's what you should be fighting for:

- Fight to preserve a friendship, not to destroy it.
- Fight to solve a problem, not to salvage your ego.
- Fight for a relationship, not against it.
- Fight for reconciliation, not for alienation.
- Fight for your spouse, not to lose him or her.
- Fight to save your marriage, not to cash it in.

If you're going to fight, fight with your heart and not your mouth.

Fighting is optional and can have damaging results that cannot ever be repaired or forgotten. So be absolutely sure that whatever you decide to fight about is worth every word and all the emotional energy you have.

Trying to be someone else is a waste of the person you are.

The Six Most Important Phrases
in a Relationship

Do you get along well in your relationship and with other people? Let's take a look.

Getting along with others is really very simple. You are polite and positive, and you don't act like a fool. Well, that's not exactly all you need if you want to be a good person and get along with others. There are no rules or requirements to having a great relationship, but there are a few common sense tactics that will take your relationship from okay to wonderful.

The countdown of the six most important phrases to say in a relationship are as follows:

6. "I made a mistake."
5. "You did a good job."
4. "What's your opinion?"
3. "Please."
2. "Thank you."
1. "We."

The least important word in any relationship is "I." There are two of you, two emotions, two sets of feelings, two hearts, two preferences, two sets of dislikes.

If you're going to be in a relationship or friendship, remember that it's not about you. It's now about both of you. It's about that word you hear all the time—*compromise!*

When you're in a situation and you don't know what to do, take the high road, be humble, and choose your words carefully. Try a few from the list above; they just might fit.

When you choose to see the good in others, you end up finding the good in yourself.

How Is Your Relationship?

At some point, it's a good idea to look at your relationships closely. Why? If your relationship means anything to you, you should you want to make sure it's going well. Look at the keys areas to ensure that you are doing what you should be doing.

So how do you think your relationship is going? Is it just all right? Is it fantastic? Does it need work? Regardless of the type of relationship you have (marriage, partnership, friendship), the following suggestions will keep it healthy:

Commitment. True commitment means much more than simply committing to the relationship. Genuine commitment involves being committed to the growth and best interests of the other person. Honesty is a must in any relationship, and if you can't commit to being open and honest, you'll never make it.

Teamwork. Use the most important sentence in any relationship: "Let's try it your way".

Communication. Every relationship has struggles with effective communication. You must be honest and open in your relationship. Hiding or omitting little things you think are unimportant may be important to the other person. If you habitually omit the "little" things, your relationship will begin to deteriorate because you will destroy your credibility. Be open and honest.

Meeting emotional needs. How do you meet your partner's emotional needs? Simple; just ask—and then be prepared for their answer. Emotional needs are about feelings, and no two people are alike when it comes to feelings. Be sensitive and respectful of his or hers.

Resolving conflict. Conflicts in a relationship are inevitable. Fighting, however, is optional. Keep your resolution at a discussion level, giving each other an uninterrupted time to freely speak. Listen to what each of you says to the other, and realize how you're perceived by each other. Never be confrontational, and never argue. All that wasted energy resolves nothing, and words can't be taken back. When things are said in anger, the damage is down.

Confrontation and arguing is a sign to stop immediately. You cannot argue about what the other person has perceived. It may not have been how you meant for something to have happened or been said, but that's the perception the other one had, which you can't change or remove.

Earlier in this book, I have given you a personal example of how not to let perceptions get out of hand with someone who was not willing to talk about anything and who only wanted to control everything including controlling me.

So how do you resolve something that's already been done? Listen to the other person's perception of the situation, without interruption, and then offer your intended meaning of what you did/said. Remember it's already done. Put the information from both sides on the table, and leave it at that. The other person now knows your initial intention, and you know his or her perception. Learn from it, let it go, and move on without holding a grudge.

Apology and forgiveness. On a regular basis, practice the three A's of a successful relationship: apologize, appreciate, and anticipate. Apologize for something from the past, appreciate something in the present, and anticipate something that will be in the future. Once you've apologized and forgiven the other person, never go back to that topic again and dig it up. You've just resolved it, so learn from it, let it go, and move on without any grudges.

Create a relationship vision. Ask yourself and each other this question: "If we knew we couldn't fail, and we could design our relationship in any way we wanted it, how would we like it to be?"

Remember that relationships are a two-way street. You both have a say, but you both need to cooperate. Start by following the suggestions I've given for keeping a relationship healthy. A relationship is a beautiful thing. Give it 100 percent—or none at all.

> *Never push a loyal person to the point where he or she no longer gives a damn.*

Do You Know What Love Really Is?

When the bottom of your world falls out and you're at rock bottom, remember that remaining at rock bottom is a choice. You do not have to stay there. You can get up, reassess, and begin the climb back up—it's your choice.

Never lose your faith, your belief in yourself, your hope, or your love.

If that comment surprises you, maybe you aren't aware of what love really is. Maybe you have the wrong idea about it.

First of all, let me tell you what love *isn't*. Love is not about sex; love is about what you feel within yourself about something or someone. Love isn't about being inseparable; it's about being true to one another when you are separated. Love isn't a choice, but staying in love is. Love isn't what you say; it's what you do.

What *is* love:

- Love is never jealous.
- Love is never envious.
- Love is never arrogant.
- Love is very patient.
- Love is always kind.
- Love is never boastful.
- Love is never selfish.
- Love is never conceited.
- Love is never rude.
- Love never demands having your own way.
- Love is not irritable or touchy.
- Love does not hold grudges.
- Love will hardly notice when others do it wrong.
- Love is never glad about injustice.
- Love celebrates whenever the truth wins out.
- Love is loyal no matter what the cost. (Dogs are the best example of this.)
- Love will always believe.
- Love will always expect only the best.

- Love will always defend.
- Love goes on forever.

Even if you're at rock bottom in your own life, you will always have faith, belief, hope and love. If you tend to run from love, you have the wrong information about what love really is. Love *is* your faith, your belief, your hope from within yourself. Get the meaning of love right, and know you always have someone to love.

Love is not what you say; love is what you do.

How to Determine What Kind of
Friend You Really Are to Others

Do you think you're a great friend? Are you really, or is that your interpretation? Are you seeing clearly the person you truly are? Believe it or not, some people think they're the greatest friends, but others see them very differently. Some think they have dozens of friends, when in reality they have dozens of acquaintances and maybe one "friend" who puts up with them. Of course, there are many types of friendly arrangements.

Do you know what it is to be a good and real friend? How would you rate yourself as a friend? Answer the following questions to help determine what type of friend you are. (Read them with an open mind, and then ask "Am I like that?")

- Do you practice unsolicited acts of kindness?
- Can you enjoy a friend's good fortune, whether in marriage, motherhood, or career, even if you aren't on a parallel track?
- Are you loyal; do you guard your friends' secrets?
- Do you encourage other people to develop their strengths and graciously help them overcome weaknesses?
- Do you refuse to become the only nurturer in the relationship?
- Can you listen when friends tell you that you've hurt them, or do you withdraw or get defensive?
- Are you a good listener, or do you claim more than your share of air time?
- Can you ask for and grant forgiveness—and mean it?
- Do you approach others with an attitude of acceptance and interest?
- Do you live an authentic life, based on your values and beliefs?
- Do you reach out to others rather than always expect that they will call or come to see you? Do you reciprocate?
- When you meet others, are you open to the possibility that they might become future allies, confidants, or best friends?

- Do you give and maintain 100 percent honesty with others, or do you withhold some of the truth?
- Do you openly admit when you are wrong without having to be caught in the act first?
- Do you listen with an open mind when you are corrected or critiqued?
- Do you give credit to the one who has helped you, or do you keep the credit for yourself?
- Do you feel equal to others, or do you feel superior to those around you?

Only you know if you were 100 percent honest with your answers. If you answered no to any of these questions, you have some work to do. You're not coming across the way you should be, or you're not listening to others. If you don't get many calls from others, chances are you're not the person you think you are. Most likely there's something abrasive or self-absorbed about you that others see.

Take an honest look at yourself, or ask someone you admire for an honest opinion—and heed that advice.

Change your thoughts, and you can change your world.

What Kind of Friend Are You?

You probably have a lot of acquaintances, but do you have several close friends or even one or two close friends? Would you row a boat for them if they asked for your help? Actually, the number of people you call "friends" has no relevance here because that is your personal business.

My point is to get you to think for a moment about those friends you do have in your life who are special and how you measure up as a friend.

Now there are about as many types of friendships as there are people, and that's fine, but are you a worthy friend? Would you want to be friends with you? Here are a few thoughts about what it takes to be a good friend:

- Be one who says positive things about others.
- Look people in the eye when you talk to them.
- Always call if you're running late.
- Don't establish a friendship based on mutual dislikes.
- Seek quiet people. They have a lot to say if you say something first.
- Make friends, even if you don't think you need them.
- Learn to tell a good story.
- Ask other people about themselves.
- Be genuinely happy for others in their good fortune.
- Make sure your caring includes doing.
- Know when to say good-bye.
- Introduce people to one another.

Being a good friend is being a good person in any type of relationship. It means honesty, communication, being positive, giving, and listening, just to name a few. As with any relationship, it can also be exhausting if it's forced and one-sided. Your friends should make you feel like a better person for knowing them and cause you to feel inspired.

Think about your situation and yourself. Do you feel good about your relationships? Can you say you are a better friend because of them?

Friends are the most important ingredient in the recipe of life.

Do You Know How to Find Support?

Let's be honest; sometimes you just need to talk. Things aren't going right, you can't concentrate, and you're not yourself. No matter what you do, you just can't think straight. You can't hold in everything; sometimes you fell that you just need to get it out or your head will explode. Be careful, though, because not everyone is the appropriate person with whom to share your inner thoughts. You may have a "gut" feeling about in whom you can (or can't) confide.

Sometimes you need to look beyond the "front row" when deciding with whom to share your concerns. When you need to find a confidant, someone to whom you can honestly vent, look for:

- someone you trust
- someone who will keep a confidence
- someone who will respect your boundaries
- someone who will pray for you
- someone who will give you perspective
- someone who is wise and has more experience than you
- someone who values commitment
- someone who will keep you accountable without unjustly condemning you
- someone of the same sex
- someone who will not be negatively affected by your confidence.

Don't suffer alone; there's no need for that. Get another perspective, an outside view from someone who will not have a bias or personal connection. This is your challenge, and how you deal with it will affect your results. Whatever you do to resolve your issues and the need for a listening ear, clear your other thoughts so you can focus on the concern at hand.

> *It's not what happens to you in life that matters. It's how you respond to what happens to you that makes the difference.*

Do You Know How to Be a Good Friend?

Even when you go through struggles, you can still be a good friend—but do you know how to be a good friend? Statistically, over 90 percent of people think they are a "good friend" to others. That confuses me because if that were true, 10 percent of people would be lonely and without a friend. That doesn't make sense to me.

That statistic really tells me that over 90 percent of people have no idea how they are perceived as a friend and most likely aren't even friend material in the first place. That might sound harsh, but think about that statistic again. Why do so many individuals face challenges alone and unhappy? A friend cannot cure all our ills, but a "good friend" can sure help us get through the major challenges in our lives. In thinking about how to be a good friend, let's break it down.

- Smile often, laugh out loud, and even giggle.
- Become aware of several things that you especially enjoy. Watch for others who enjoy those same things.
- Identify an acquaintance who has a need you can help with, and then offer yourself as help.
- Learn to enjoy being alone. Identify what parts of living enrich your life and incorporate them in your daily routines. If you find you are happy being with yourself, it's likely others will enjoy your company too.
- Forget what you give, remember what you receive, but never keep score.
- Be the one who is there *doing* when others are still saying; "Is there anything I can do?" If you have to ask, you are not a true friend.
- Listen, even in the silence.

Do you do any of these things naturally? Are you a good friend? If you are, you're amazing, and your friend thanks you. If you're not, try a few of the suggestions in the above list, and make them a habit every day.

Be to someone, how you would want them to be to you

CHAPTER 5

Family

Dealing with family issues is daunting for some and exhilarating for other. Regardless of where you fit, your family is your blood and soul, and how you deal with them will affect everything you do in life. This chapter is meant to help you see all sides of your family members, from young to old, as well as how others perceive you and your family.

"I Hate You!"

If you are a parent and your child has spoken those three words to you, or if you ever said those words to your parent at some point, you'll identify with what I'm about to share.

After spending my nursing career of taking care of patients, I've had thousands of conversations with them and have heard their honesty when no one else is around. Regardless of their ages, their words were real, candid, and from the heart as they expressed their feelings.

People often have something on their minds and only need someone to listen and hear what they are saying. Children have no fear when expressing themselves and have the least amount of hesitation about speaking what's on their minds, especially when they have no one to filter their thoughts. I want to share a collection of some of those candid thoughts from children.

The following comments are unedited; they're the actual words from children ages four through eighteen, although some sentences have been revised for clarification purposes only.

- Don't forget how quickly I'm growing up. It must be very difficult for you to keep up with me, but please try.
- Don't nag all the time. If you do, I will have to protect myself by appearing deaf.
- Don't put me off when I ask questions. If you do, you will find that I stop asking, and I'll find my information somewhere else.
- Don't correct me in front of people, please. I'll take more notice if you talk to me quietly in private,
- Don't be so inconsistent. That completely confuses me and makes me lose faith in you.
- Don't spoil me. I know that I shouldn't have everything I ask for. I'm just testing you.
- Don't forget I need lots of love and understanding.
- Don't make rash promises. Remember, I feel badly let down when promises are broken.
- Don't protect me from consequences. I need to learn the painful way sometimes.
- Don't make me feel smaller than I am. It only makes me behave like a stupid big person.
- Don't forget I can't explain myself as well as I want to. That's why I'm not always very accurate.
- Don't be afraid to be firm with me. I prefer that; it makes me feel more secure.
- Don't tell me my fears are silly. They are terribly real, and you can do so much.
- Don't let me form bad habits. I rely on you to see them and correct them early on.
- Don't think it's beneath you to apologize to me. You teach me to be honest and apologize when I'm wrong. I know you aren't perfect, and if you apologize to me too when you are wrong, it would make me feel so warm with you.
- Don't get too upset with my small boo-boos. Sometimes they get me the attention I need.

- Don't ever suggest you are perfect or never make mistakes. It's too shocking for me when I discover you are neither.
- Don't be too upset when I say "I hate you." It isn't you I hate, but you power-block me when I want to do something.

These expressions are just a sampling of the thousands of thoughts that really stuck out in my mind. Children have no fear of speaking their minds. Maybe adults should start expressing themselves as honestly as the children.

The way we talk to our children becomes their inner voices.

"My Mom and Dad Just Don't Get Me!"

Have you ever heard those words from a child? I know I have. Some children never say anything about frustrations they may have, but many do. Do your children, grandchildren, nieces, or nephews have a voice? Do they express their feelings?

This next list is what I call the Child's Ten Commandments to Parents. It's a collection of children's comments using their words, their thoughts, their points of view regarding their parents, activities, chores, and life in general.

Here are some thoughts from the "mouths of babes":

Commandment 1
Please be sensitive to my needs. My feelings are tender. Don't nag me all day long. (You wouldn't want to be nagged for your curiosity.) Treat me as you would like to be treated.

Commandment 2
Please let me explore safely. My eyes have not seen the world as yours have. Don't restrict me unnecessarily.

Commandment 3
Please don't expect perfection whenever I make a bed, draw a picture, or throw a ball; my hands are small. Please slow down so that I can keep up with you; my legs are short.

Commandment 4
Please go easy on the criticism. Remember, you can criticize the things I do without criticizing me. I need your encouragement to grow.

Commandment 5
Please give me the freedom to make decisions concerning myself. Permit me to fail so that I can learn from my mistakes. Then, someday, I'll be prepared to make the kinds of decisions life requires of me.

Commandment 6

Please treasure me as God intended you to do; I am a special gift from God. Hold me accountable for my actions, give me guidelines to live by, and discipline me in a loving manner.

Commandment 7

Please take time to explain things to me about this wonderful world, and do so willingly. Housework will always be there, I'm little for such a short time.

Commandment 8

Please don't do things over for me. Somehow that makes me feel that my efforts didn't quite measure up to your expectations. I know it's hard, but please don't try to compare me with my brother, or sister, or anyone else.

Commandment 9

Please take me to Sunday school and church regularly. Set a good example for me to follow. I enjoy learning, even though I don't like getting dressed up.

Commandment 10

Please don't be afraid to leave for a weekend together. Kids need vacations from parents, just as parents need vacations from kids. Besides, it's a great way to show us kids that your marriage is very special and that you trust us.

These common thoughts from children of all ages were expressed in a way they understand with regard to the cues, messages, and correction they receive from their parents. I'm *not* saying that parents or adults shouldn't discipline, guide, teach, or show responsibility to their children. Children must have discipline as they grow, and that is the responsibility of the parent(s). The Child's Ten Commandments to Parents, however, offers their children's perspective—their feelings.

Your mind is the garden & your thoughts are the seeds.
You can choose to grow flowers, or you can grow weeds

Do You Know What to Ask Elderly Parents or Grandparents?

I've been in these uncomfortable situations, and it's not easy, like the commercials show on television. I'm referring to talking about death. I can tell you, however, that if you don't talk about this subject with your parents or grandparents to get some clarity, the issues that you will face after they're gone will be very difficult and can cost you a lot of money.

I've spent my career dealing with life-or-death situations and everything that goes with it, so I'll be blunt about some things. If you don't address these questions, I can assure you that you will go through a massive roll of red tape. Even if your family situation is such that this doesn't pertain to you (your elder adults are already deceased, for example), you may have relatives who are still living or family or friends who may benefit from this information.

The following list suggests questions to ask of elderly parents or grandparents and includes city, state and government requirements:

- Do you have an attorney?
- Do you have an up-to-date will?
- Do you have any hidden assets or liabilities?
- Where do you keep your important financial documents?
- Who will handle your affairs if you become incapacitated?
- Do you have a living will?
- Do you have a medical power of attorney?
- Do you have sufficient medical insurance?
- Do you have long-term care insurance?
- Have you made funeral plans?
- Will your estate owe taxes, and do you have money to pay them?
- Do you have an administrator of the estate?

Most of us don't want to bring up these points, much less get in an involved discussion, but I cannot stress enough the urgency of dealing with the matter of these documents and having a conversation now—don't put it off for any reason.

Without these basic documents, drawn up by an attorney and kept on file, as well as kept in a place where you can find them quickly and easily, you will have a difficult situation on your hands.

You cannot change what you refuse to confront.

I Have No Idea How to Help My Parents"

Here are simple ways that adult children can help their parents or elderly relatives. First, ask yourself if you *don't know how* to help your parents or if you *don't want* to help your parents. This is reality. We think our parents will be around forever, but they won't. Your parents or elderly relatives are aging, and they do need you, whether they admit it or not. From medical professional's point of view, the more you are involved in their care, the more the medical staff can do for them and help them to stay as viable as possible.

Here are simple ways for adult children to help aging parents or relatives:

- Stimulate their social lives. Encourage them to maintain old social relationships and to make new ones. This is a time when they need old friends.
- Encourage reminiscing. Draw memories of the past and help them fit together the pieces of the experiences.
- Support usefulness. Ask them for advice, praise their hobbies, and encourage their giving service to others.
- Support "letting go." Help them find constructive ways to dispose of possessions by discussing how thrift stores and mission programs can benefit from their contributions. Take the time to listen to them and cry with them when they have to give up their homes, their driver's licenses, or their leadership positions.
- Encourage spiritual growth. Help them find large-print Bibles and enriching TV and radio programs. Help them find transportation to attend church. Encourage them to join a prayer group or chain or a service group.
- Respect independence. For as long as possible, your parents need to make their own decisions about where and how to live.
- Listen to them. Listen and hear the accounts of their past disappointments, accomplishments, and satisfactions, even if told repeatedly. Also, listen to the accounts of their current worries, fears, joys, hopes, and delights.

- Communicate often. Keep in touch by telephone, visits, and letters. Remember holidays, birthdays, and anniversaries.
- Pray for them and with them. Their physical, mental, social, and material well-being is interconnected with their spiritual health.

Your parents brought you the gift of life. Ignoring them now is hugely disrespectful to them, to your responsibility, and to God. Regardless of the relationship you've had with them, now is not the time to turn your back on them, especially if they are a bit confused, forgetful, or constantly repeat things. Remember that when they reach this point, they are trapped inside a body they no longer recognize, and they may not fully understand what's happened to them. They aren't acting like this to irritate you; they're scared and unable to understand this strange world and why their known surroundings are gone.

If you visit them out of obligation or a sense of duty, or if you act irritated and preoccupied while you're with them, they will sense this and know you don't want to be there.

No one wants to go through this, no one want to be like that, and no one wants to be treated as if they're nobody. Spend time with your parents when you can. They're going through a process that has no instructions and no reasoning, and they're terrified.

Be their rock; after all, they were your rock when you were growing up.

> *People don't always need advice. Sometimes all they need is a hand to hold, an ear to listen, and a heart to understand them.*

How to Recognize Where Your Money Is Going

Are you one of the millions of people whose money seems to drain from your wallet?

You do your best; you go shopping, and all of a sudden you end up with all this *stuff*, and your money's gone! You may have thought you were being careful—you shopped with a list—but what happened? Or maybe you went to the store for one thing—just *one darn thing*—but ended up with a buggy full of stuff? Unless you go shopping with blinders on, you'll look around and see items that are not on your list. Many people (although I think it's women more than men) just "go shopping" for social fun. (Men don't say to their buddies, "Hey, let's have lunch on Saturday and go shopping.")

Taking a list is a good start, and sticking to your list is great, but the key is being consistent every time you go to the store. Here are my suggestions on spending and being more frugal with money.

- The more you read magazines, newspaper advertisements, and grocery store flyers, the more you spend.
- The more time you spend looking through catalogs, the more you spend.
- The more you watch television commercials, the more you spend.
- The more shopping you do, the more you spend.

These are only four keys to spending too much that most people don't usually think about.

We already know the basics:

- Don't grocery shop on an empty stomach.
- Don't eat out more than once a week.
- Don't shop without a list, and strictly follow that list.
- Only go to the store when you have a large enough list, not every other day.
- Leave your children at home or with a sitter or family member.
- Choose store brands instead of the top brands.

- Do not cut back on your pet's food; cut back on your own food.
- Buy what you need, not what you want.

Use common sense and remember that you are the only one who can control what you spend. It's all on you.

If you really want to do something, you'll find a way.
If you don't, you'll find an excuse.

Happy Fourth of July, America!

What a glorious day—family, friends, gatherings, picnics, cookouts, a day of special celebrations. We love this holiday! It's about freedom, love, gratitude, appreciation, stories, and laughter. But it's really about those who gave their lives to give America freedom centuries ago.

Here's what the day should and should not mean to you.

The Fourth of July *should* mean:

- gratitude
- appreciation
- giving
- military veterans
- forgiveness

The Fourth *should not* mean:

- resentment
- anger
- bad attitudes
- grudges

On this day, sincerely thank a veteran. Remember those veterans with post-traumatic stress disorder (PTSD). Fireworks, firecrackers, and other noisy celebrations are very traumatic to those with PTSD.

Remember your dogs and cats and those of your neighbors. Fireworks, firecrackers, and other noisy celebrations are very traumatic to animals.

Remember safety first for you, your family, and those around you. Emergency rooms around the country have an incredibly high rate of injuries on this day. So many injuries are preventable. Please use caution!

Embrace the day of celebration and be safe.

Have a Memorable Mother's Day

On Mother's Day, I hope you wished your mom, mum, mother, ma, and yourself a wonderful and happy Mother's Day. On the day before Mother's Day, I heard someone say, "Every day is Mother's Day. Why is tomorrow any different?"

My mother is no longer living, and to hear a comment like that hit me like an arrow through my heart. I felt myself go cold; I just stood there as my mind played a collage of memories of the special days we always had for her.

My earliest memory of Mother's Day for my mom was my giving her a bouquet of flowers I had picked for her the day before. I could hardly keep my mouth shut about it because I was so proud that I'd done it all by myself. On the morning of Mom's special day, I remember Dad saying to me, "Let's go outside a minute." I eagerly ran out the door in my bare feet after him. I knew whenever we went somewhere, he would show me something new, and oh, how I loved being with him. Dad was so smart; he even knew how to put a worm on a hook so it would stay on and not wiggle off, like when I did it. How I wished to be smart like him when I grew up.

I followed Dad like a puppy out into the backyard. He went into the big shed off the garage, where I was hiding Mom's gift. He picked up my flowers and knelt beside me. He said, "What do you think, Lin? They look a little tired this morning. How about if I go with you to where you got these. You can pick out some more flowers for Mom that are more awake than this bouquet." Well, I had to think about it for a minute, but then I beamed. I thought, *What a great idea. Mom will be so happy with awake flowers.*

Off we went, Dad and I, so I could show him my special place where I'd picked Mom's flowers yesterday. When we got there, I pointed to the fence by the water, where there were flowers that looked so beautiful and awake! I ran ahead and started picking more flowers right away, thinking, *Dad was right. These do look more awake this morning than the ones I picked yesterday.* I kept picking and picking, making the biggest bouquet I'd ever seen. *Thanks, Dad. You are so smart and know more than just hooking worms for fishing!*

Beaming with excitement, I couldn't wait to get back home to give Mom my present. *She's going to be so happy,* I thought. But Dad told me, "I have an idea." Dad always had the best ideas. As we got closer to our house, we crossed over to one of Dad's gardens (he had two huge gardens) and stopped. He looked down at the patch of asparagus and said, "What do you think, Lin?"

"Oh yeah," I said as we both got down on the ground and started picking and cutting fresh asparagus. Dad always had his pocket knife with him, and I too had the tiny one he gave me in my pocket, just like him. Finally, Dad said, "You think we have enough?"

"Yup," I said, "let's go. Mom is going to love this—her favorites: asparagus and flowers!"

I was just bursting I was so proud of my gift to Mom, and she was so surprised when I gave her my big bouquet of flowers. She smiled and gave me one of her big warm hugs while whispering, "I love you, sweetie," in my ear like she always did. She took my huge bouquet of "awake" dandelions, put them in her best vase, and set them in the middle of the dinner table for everyone to see. I was so excited to see Mom fuss over those flowers I'd picked for her that I could barely eat ...

Suddenly, I heard something from a distance and noticed someone talking right there in front of me. "Hey, lady, are you all right?"

I looked at the man who'd just said, "Every day is Mother's Day ..." and realized I had been daydreaming about one of my mom's many Mother's Days—the very first one I could remember. That day is still so vivid in my memory, like so many we had together in our happy house. I thought about that all night. I will never have those days again to celebrate Mother's Day. I will never be able to feel her energy, to see the smile on her face, to feel the big warm hugs she always gave, to have that wonderful scent of her soaps and lotions fill the air like a colorful scented garden, or hear her whisper in my ear, "I love you sweetie."

My mom is no longer here with us. She died in 1995, four years after my dad, the love of her life. I tell this story as a tribute because of a story I heard from a dear friend from New Zealand. My friend is truly a remarkable woman. She did something that freed her heart and soul from all the toxic rot that had built up within her. She had a wonderful breakthrough with her own mum when she reached out and called her mum on Mother's Day to tell her she loved her. Despite the years of choppy ground, this wonderful woman initiated the contact to reunite with her mum. She did this after her husband told her five words that made so much sense: "Just do it for you."

Not everyone has happy memories of his or her mother. Not everyone has a relationship with his or her mother, for whatever reason. Not everyone's mother is still alive.

But regardless of your situation, you have the power to "just do it for you." Regardless of your current issues, pick up a phone and call your mother, or look her in the eye, or look up to the heavens and say, "Happy Mother's Day. I love you, and I miss you."

There is nothing like the love of a mother.

How to Pull Off the Best Surprises

Most people do love surprises. The fact that someone thought about you and took the time to do something nice or even wacky for another person means a lot. (If it doesn't, then you're a work in progress.)

Some parents have fun ideas to surprise their children. As those children become adults themselves they can then use those same fun ideas their own kids, grandkids, husband, wife, partner, or friends. I think most of us like to do something fun, out of character, or over the top and silly—without breaking the law. You can only work so much, and there comes a time on any given day when you want to do something that might actually make you or someone else laugh.

So how do you pull off the best surprises? The following suggestions will give you some ideas:

Surprise party: Whether it's a birthday, special occasion, or no reason at all, throw a surprise party. Make a cake, hang decorations, and invite friends. Just talke the time to create a fun surprise will be enough to make it memorable.

Notes tucked away: Write an encouraging note to each of your children, your mate, or your friend. Put the notes in their lunch boxes, tool box, purse, wallet, or car. If you're really creative and have time, draw a little cartoon. An unexpected positive word can sometimes make a memory that lasts a lifetime.

Kids or mate "In-Charge Night": Put your kids, grandkids, or mate in charge for a day. Let them choose what you'll do in the afternoon, and then ask them to set the table and give them simple recipes to cook for dinner (if they don't already have a favorite meal to cook). Use any easy menu like spaghetti or pancakes, and let them go at it. The lesson will be worth the mess! After dinner, guide kids or grandkids through washing dishes, sorting laundry, emptying trash, and sewing on buttons. During the activities, talk with them about the importance of fulfilling responsibilities.

Scavenger hunt: Wake up your kids, grandkids, or mate or call your friend one morning and announce they have an important task after breakfast. Tell them they have two hours to find everything on your list (a red button, a yellow rose, a stuffed animal, two joker cards, a picture of a mountain, a penny from the 1970s, a mattress advertisement, or whatever you want to include—the sillier the better). The fun is in the hunt. At the end of the game, it's also fun for everyone to tell the story of what they went through to find everything on the list. Award a prize to the winner—the choice is up to you.

Water fight: When was the last time you asked your kids or anyone to help you wash the car and then got everyone into a water fight? It might seem silly, but it's also a riot. They will talk about that water fight for years to come. The chance for the kids to see their parents, siblings, and friends have silly fun is priceless.

Pajama ride: One night while the kids or grandkids and their sleep-over friends are in their pajamas and tucked into bed, wait about ten minutes and then race into their room, flip on the light, and yell, "Pajama ride!" Wrap a blanket around them, put them in the car, and go for ice cream at Dairy Queen or another drive-up ice cream stand. Your pajama ride will show them your spontaneous side, and everyone will treasure this memory of seeing you act crazy! *Build a fort*: Take the time to build something with your special person or kids. Build a living room fort of cushions and blankets, a tree fort, a backyard tent—whatever it is that you can do together. There is something about the memory of working together and building a structure that especially stays with kids. It'll also give you time to talk about what's going on in their lives.

Day off from school or work: One day, after one of your kids has received a good report card or after your mate or friend has done something exceptionally nice for you, show up at school or their workplace. Say, "I'm sorry, but I have to take you out of school [or work] today, I need you to do something important with me." Then take them to lunch, a movie, to a museum, the zoo, a flea market, fishing, or whatever you choose. Sometimes a day with you is more important than a day with the teacher or boss. If you can't make it an entire day, then make it a lunch date! That will be a memory that'll last a lifetime.

That is how to pull off the best surprises. Some may seem goofy, but it's not as easy to make lasting memories out of mundane daily t routines. You make memories out of the times and the laughter you have together while doing things and seeing a side of someone that is totally unexpected. Make the times in your life worth remembering, and you'll have lived life to the fullest.

> *"It's not the years in your life that count; it's the life in your years."*
>
> —Abraham Lincoln

How to Welcome a New Neighbor Right from the Start

It seems that many people's biggest fear is getting new neighbors. What will they be like? Will they be loud or park their cars and trucks all over their lawn? Do they have a loud barking dog? Whether you're in an apartment, condo, or a house, everyone worries about the "newbies" moving in next door. Why is that? At some point, other people tolerated your moving into the neighborhood.

As with everything else, first impressions are important. So be careful and do it right because you won't have a second chance to make a good impression. Here's how to welcome a new neighbor properly, right from the start:

- Strongly resist the urge to stand at your window to watch them move in. While they unload the truck, trailer, and vehicles, don't stare at them. They will see you and think you're very rude.
- Acknowledge that you see the moving van. Give a wave of your hand from your yard, or a call out a quick, "Welcome to the neighborhood" or "I'm looking forward to meeting you." Do *not*, however, go over there while they're moving in. They don't have time for you then, and you will look like you only want to see the inside of their house.
- Drop off a plate of cookies or a pot of stew. These can be most appreciated at the front door, but don't go in unless they invite you in. Then stay only a few minutes unless they ask for your help and are welcome.
- After you've read your local newspaper, leave them your copy in their mailbox or on their porch for the first week. The paper will help to get them orientated to your area and city.
- If the neighbors are from out of town, make a packet for them with a city map, a list of local events (such as concerts), or points of local interest (such as museums), Or, with their permission, give their name and address to a local welcoming service.

- If the new neighbors' children or pets violate your space, make your boundaries known—but blend firmness with kindness. If you don't complain about their dog pottying in your yard when it first begins, the habit will become difficult to break.
- Tell neighbors to let you know if they need recommendations for shopping, a dentist, dry cleaners, and so forth, rather than just volunteering the information.
- Never be critical of the people who lived in the new neighbors' house before them. Trashing someone else will immediately tell them the type of person you are.
- After two weeks, have a neighborhood dessert party or potluck dinner at your house. You can introduce the newcomers to others who live nearby.
- If your offer of help or friendship is refused, don't push. Wait until your neighbors have time to get settled and look you over. In the meantime, just smile genuinely.

Give your new neighbors space and time. Moving to a new area is very stressful, and organizing and settling into a new home can be overwhelming for many people. No two people unpack and settle in the same way, and of course their schedules may also be new. After an initial wave or hello, give them a month or more before you start knocking on their door, unless you are specifically invited to visit.

Remember again—you have only one chance to make an inviting good impression. Use the chance wisely.

Be kind. Everyone you meet is fighting a battle you know nothing about.

How You Can Regain Cooperation from Your Children

"My kids are so out of control!" Does this sound familiar to you? It should because it does seem that children are out of control today. The only one who has the right to control your
kids or grandchildren is you. Where does this out-of-control behavior come from? It's from lack of respect and communication, on both sides.

So, instead of dwelling on what we know, let's talk about some ideas to help this issue. I've compiled a few thoughts for families that might set things in motion.

It starts with communication between you and your children and an agreement that you'll work on these together.

Family commitments

o   If I make a mess, I'll clean it up.
o   I will treat others with respect.
o   I'll pick up my clothes and keep my room neat.
o   I will not use bad language.
o   I will not lie.
o   I will not keep secrets.
o   I will not hit others.
o   I'll talk to Mom, Dad, or my grandparents about my problems.
o   I'll do my chores and homework before I go out to play.
o   I will not use drugs, and if I know somebody who is using drugs, I'll find them help at home.
o   I will turn off my phone during all mealtimes.

These types of commitments may vary, depending on your particular situation, but they do work. The key is to discuss them with your children. These are called teachable moments. It's your opportunity to work together on these issues and made an agreement to do these faithfully.

The commitments listed above are not to just so you can "get control" of your children. Your children should carry on with them throughout their lives.

"How wonderful it is that nobody needs wait a single moment before starting to improve the world"
—Anne Frank

The Best Qualities to Pass on to Your Kids

Regardless of what type of family atmosphere you were brought up in, you cannot use "I wasn't raised that way" as an excuse. Qualities are learned, and anyone at any time can learn to adopt good qualities. If you know you lack the basic qualities, you can still develop them. How?

You have to *want* to be a good person. You have to *want* to do the right things. You have to *want* to change yourself. You must believe in these qualities. You make a conscious effort to develop and practice these qualities every day. You do *not* use these once in a while. They must be part of your personality and part of who you are, and they must come from your heart.

Do you want to be a better person? Do you want to pass good qualities on to your children and others? Here's a list of the best of those qualities:

- o Self-control: when under stress, stay calm.
- o Patience: fight irritability. Be willing to wait.
- o Compassion: when another hurts, feel it with him or her.
- o Diligence: work hard. Tough it out.
- o Determination: stick with it, regardless.
- o Honesty: speak and live the truth—always.
- o Responsibility: be dependable and trustworthy.
- o Thoughtfulness: think of others before yourself.
- o Confidentiality: don't tell secrets. Seal your lips.
- o Punctuality: be on time.
- o Purity: reject anything that lowers your standards.

You can be a lot of things in life, and you can pass on a lot of things to your children. But qualities like these are the makeup of a truly good person.

If you already have these qualities, I'm very proud of you. If you're lacking any of these qualities, it's never too late to develop them by starting today.

Truly good people are hard to find, but they're out there, and they are wonderful to be around. I have been blessed abundantly by wonderful people from all over the world who have become incredible friends. I wouldn't trade them for anything on this earth. When you have quality people in your life, you truly are at peace. I know I am.

When you feel like you cannot go another step, that's
when you give it everything you've got ...

How to Create a Teamwork Skill at Home

Recently, while out walking as part of my therapy, I ran into wonderful neighbors I hadn't seen since my accident. Their kids had grown, and their one dog was now two dogs. A lot of energy was going on. The wife held back from her "pack" a little and said to me, "Oh my gosh, they're driving me crazy already, and school is just about to be out for the summer. What am I going to do?" She laughed as she spoke, so I knew she wasn't serious. She's such a good mom and wife. Still, this was a surprising remark, even said kiddingly, from a woman who's generally very laid back and soft-spoken. I laughed with her but could see what was coming in that household and many others.

When you think about it, most families have these issues year-round, so it got me thinking about backup plans. What can you do with your family, regardless of whether you're in a traditional family, single parent, new parent, or have relatives you care for? The following information pertains to everyone, regardless of their status. In fact, if you are having a rough time right now, this is the best information for you.

Team building

- Work together: assign chores that must be completed with cooperation.
- Great goals: promote activities where siblings must work together to reach a goal.

Charity work

- Encourage your kids to reach out to the less fortunate and help them in their yards.

Games

During family time, join the kids as a team. The quality time is amazing.

Fun projects

- Promote sibling activities, like large puzzles, making birdhouses, or craft kits, to develop a sense of teamwork. Use limited supplies of glue and markers so the children must share.

Offering for every occasion

- Unite all ideas to create gifts, such as cookies for neighbors or presents for grandparents that they have made themselves.

Book time

- Have children read to each other, or have an older child read to a younger sibling. Also, make up your own sibling stories for your kids. Have a Super Brother save little sister from the scary bear, or even add your children as characters in Bible stories.

King or queen for the day

- One day a week, have "Royal Kid Day." One child is the king or queen and receives special treatment. The other "servant" children will also enjoy themselves as they prepare food and games for the king or queen of that day. Don't forget the parents or mates can be the king or queen for the day.

Special parent day

- Siblings will have a ton of fun working together to fulfill the needs of the chosen adult. This also works great for the adults too.

Family talent night

- Encourage each child to shine like a star in front of the family with tumbling acts, singing specials, or the presentation of a school projects. These and others will bring applause and support from siblings. The catch is that the parents must also participate in talent night. Quality time spent like this will create lifetime memories. This also keeps the TV off and everyone off their devices.

These activities are meant to bring bonding, trust, teamwork, laughter, silliness, and quality activities on a budget for everyone. The best part is that it creates memories to share and talk about forever. We spend our lives trying to be grown up, so why not be a kid again and improve your health and your disposition as well.

Those with children have a limited time with them to make a difference, so use your time well.

Nothing in life has any meaning, except the meaning and memories we give it.

What Kind of Imagination Do You Have?

Not everyone is in the position to buy the latest clothes, toys, and furniture. I can certainly relate to those days, but you don't have to. Are there things you would like to have but can't buy? I get that, and it's hard to always sacrifice and go without. But it's even harder to have to say no to your kids when you're going through rough times because they don't understand.

You just might *not* have to say no to your kids, however, if you use your imagination. I'm going to dig deep here to help you look like a hero to your kids, but there is a catch. You must do one thing—you must have an open mind.

As much as commercials and ads would like you to believe it, the high cost of something does not mean it's the very best toy or item for your kids. Remember the old story told about Christmas—"Yeah, the kids got all the latest toys and wound up playing with the boxes."

Well, there is a lot of truth to that. The actual toy or object is not what is best about having it; it's the imagination in that item that makes it the best.

Here are examples of free toys or other items for children:

- A pretend post office, stocked with your old junk mail.
- Puppets made from stray socks that have piled up in your laundry room.
- Tub toys, made from empty squeeze bottles.
- A cape made from a beach towel or bath towel.
- An arm sling made from a dish towel.
- A pretend grocery store, stocked with empty food packages (cleaned soup and vegetable cans, cereal boxes, spice bottles).
- Binoculars made from empty toilet paper tubes taped together (add plastic-wrap lenses for a professional look).
- A tent made from couch cushions, sheets, and blankets (don't forget the flashlight).
- Sewing cards made from cleaned Styrofoam meat trays and old shoelaces.

- A house made from a large, empty cardboard box.
- Imagination—from books obtained with their own library card (their own name on it).

There are literally hundreds of free things for kids, but the greatest gift of value you're giving them is *imagination*. Their minds will grow, they can't break it, they can't lose it, and no one can steal it.

Look around and think like a child. Ask yourself, "What could I do with this to make it fun and build in my imagination?"

Money cannot buy memories, but memories can be made from your creative imagination.

The way we talk to and give to our children becomes their inner voice forever.

When Is the Last Time You Acted Like a Kid?

When it's family time, the things you have planned might not work out the way you'd hoped Sometimes saying "What do you want to do today" can be hard to pull off at the last second when you're not prepared or don't have the money to spend. Even worse, when you're going through rough and challenging times, it's extremely hard to even consider spending money on an activity—but maybe not.

Whether your down, on a depressed budget, or your situation is much different, you have to pull your children toward you because they don't understand what's wrong. Seeing you torn up, watching you grieve, and watching you scrape by puts an enormous amount of stress on them. Kids watch everything, and they're affected by everything you do and feel. When you're going through issues, it makes them feel like it's their fault. When they see you struggling, unhappy, negative, or broke, they want to help; they want to spend time with you, regardless of how happy or sad you are. You must give them the time they need, and don't delay until they never want to be around you.

Here are ideas to do with your kids that are mostly low cost; your kids or grandkids will love to be included.

o   Bake cookies.
o   Help a neighbor.
o   Create a poster or a painting.
o   Put on a puppet show or play.
o   Enjoy nature: put up a bird feeder, collect bugs, look at the cloud shapes, study the stars.
o   Visit a zoo, museum, or farm with animals.
o   Find something to collect; coins, rocks, marbles, baseball cards, shells.
o   Plant a garden or flowers.
o   Collect bottles, cans, and recyclables, and give the money to a charity they choose.
o   Fly a kite they have chosen.

o   Take flowers or a plant and a card to someone who is lonely or sick.
o   Read books out loud.
o   Draw picture with chalk on your driveway or sidewalk.
o   Jump rope.
o   Play hopscotch.
o   Put on a talent show.
o   Tell stories.
o   Make a fort in the living room with blankets.
o   Make family cards for Christmas, birthdays, Thanksgiving, and Valentine's Day.
o   Paint each other's faces.
o   Sing songs or make up songs.
o   Take a ride in the country to see the farms. Then stop to ask if your child can sit on the tractor or help feed a cow.
o   Help to clean up the lakeshore or beach.
o   Go swimming together.

There are hundreds of things your kids or grandkids can do, but doing these things *with you* makes it a hundred times better and more memorable. Everything you do something with your child or grandchild, it's an awesome teachable moment that will be cherished forever. Don't let these opportunities pass by. These activities may sound corny to you, but to a child, they're priceless!

> *Beautiful things happen when you view life through the eyes of children.*

Seriously, You Allow Your Child to Do That?

As a continuing part of my physical therapy, I walked outside to increase my strength, endurance, and balance. I walked every day. Recently, I decided to walk around my city, which is a tourist town and always packed in the summer. It attracts people of all ages, who come for the beautiful lake activities—from the elderly who have walkers and canes (I can relate) to the young who are excited to be on vacation. Walking slowly gives me the opportunity to observe more of what's going on around me. I'd like to share an observation I've made that seems to have been overlooked by parents—children who lack of proper manners.

I wonder what will happen to our world when these children who are out of control grow to up and are of the age to run it. I would guess that everyone has witnessed children getting away with antics while their parents ignore the behavior.

Here are my thoughts on the important manners to teach your children:

- o   Courtesy and respect to elders and authority figures
- o   Proper conduct in public places (including church)
- o   Good (not perfect) table manners
- o   Not standing on chairs, crawling on tables, or screaming
- o   Proper telephone talk and manners
- o   Meeting and greeting people properly
- o   Good verbal manners (for example, "yes" or "yes ma'am," not "yeah" or a grunt.
- o   "Hello, thank you, please, excuse me, I'm sorry, may I" are appropriate.
- o   Opening doors for others.
- o   Being a gracious host and a welcome guest.

Learning manners and appropriate behavior is important for children. I recently witnessed a child so unruly and ignored by the parent that another guest became observably upset and had to leave because of a panic attack.

Panic attacks are very real and are triggered by many different reasons. The same can be said of those suffering from post-traumatic stress disorder. You may never know their triggers.

So parents, please teach these important manners to your children. You love your children; I get that. We all love our kids. When you're in public, however, you have a responsibility to everyone, including your child, to have control and authority over your offspring and raise them with good manners. Only then we can all coexist together.

What you allow, is what will continue

How to Take Responsibility
for Your Own Children

I'm sure you've witnessed the out-of-control child in a store or restaurant. But where's the parent when the little bundle of joy is turned around and standing on the booth seat, with ketchup all over his hands, playing with your hair?

This situation actually happened to me and the child's mother never intervened.

Where's the parent when a child is screaming in the store aisle, on the floor, pulling stuff off the shelves, while looking directly at you like you caused her to spin out of control?

Yes, that was another real situation for me.

The parents usually are ignoring their children and continuing their conversations, or they keep on shopping down the aisle ahead of the trail of scattered merchandise all over the floor.

I've also had to deal with children countless times when they've come into the ER or the clinic exam rooms. I'm not talking about the kids who are patients; I can handle those just fine. I'm referring to the siblings or the kids who accompany a parent who is sick.

I've seen them come flying in the door and immediately open every cabinet door and drawer and start unloading them. Then they move to the gloves and start pulling them out faster than a machine, and then they pull things off the walls. It sounds unbelievable, but it's true.

As the years have gone by, this issue has become worse and worse. Why? Apparently parental discipline has evolved to a theoretical reasoning of sorts. I, for one, can tell you that theoretical reasoning did not keep the ketchup out of my hair or the hands with gravy off my shoulders. Nor did theoretical reasoning keep all the medical supplies off the floor of the hospital or clinic in the first fifteen seconds after their arrival.

So, let's get back to the basics—Parenting 101.

The following is the job of the parent:

o   train
o   shape
o   mold
o   correct
o   guide
o   punish
o   reward
o   instruct
o   warn
o   teach
o   discipline
o   watch at all times
o   love

Take responsibility while raising your children. It's not your child's teacher's role, it's not your family's role, and it's not an innocent bystander's role or the general public's role. It is solely the parents' responsibility to raise their children and include the basics I've mentioned above.

Until your children are finally in college or wherever they go as adults, theoretical reasoning is not how babies, children, or young adults are wired to receive and understand. On behalf of everyone in the world, please take your role and job as a parent seriously and dutifully. Please respect those around your child and respect the property around your child.

Let me share this true story with you:

My nursing pin, which I received upon graduation from college nursing school, has a very thick, very ornate style, which at first glance resembles sort of a sheriff's badge but not as large. Because I'm proud of my profession, I wear over my heart on my scrubs.

One day, a very out-of-control, unruly little four-year-old came running into the room with his ill mother. He was pulling at and throwing things everywhere. Finally, this little tornado turned around and looked up at me—and stood frozen in his tracks. With his mouth open wide, he just stared at me. The momentary silence after the screaming and running was wonderful, so I selfishly soaked it up and enjoyed the moment, while directing my attention to his very sick mother.

Finally, the little boy said very softly and seriously, while still looking up staring at me, "Are you the sheriff?"

For whatever reason at that moment, I looked back at him and replied, "Yes, I am!" The little boy never took his eyes off me, and after a five-second stare-down, he backed up slowly to a chair and never said another word for the next hour as I treated his mama.

Finally, when his mother was ready to go home, the little boy stopped at the door as they were leaving. He then turned around and looked up at me for a few seconds, and without saying a word, he saluted me like a soldier. Then he took his mama's hand and left with her.

Was it wrong of me to let that little boy think I was something I wasn't? In this situation, when there wasn't time for explanation, I think not. Thankfully, that little boy's imagination or something he'd seen triggered a memory of respect and carried it out. He'd related my 1.5-inch diameter nursing pin to an authority figure and he was smart enough to know what that meant. That little guy was definitely trainable; I only hope his mother realized it.

I do think she did realize it, because before they left, she hugged me and said quietly, "Thank you for quieting him down."

Find the blessing in everything ...

How to Be a Parent with These Easy Steps

"I don't know how to be a parent!" We've all known someone who's made this statement—maybe it was you. Or maybe it was a friend or family member who was suddenly torn between excitement and fear. Now you're responsible for another being, whether it's your biological child, a stepchild, a niece, a nephew, or a close friend. Even "parents" of a "fur baby" can modify these super-easy ideas for their parenting situations.

There are numerous parenting books out there, from *Parenting 101* to *The XYZ of Raising Kids*. Unless you memorize those books or have a psychology consultant living with you, parenting is complicated, so I'll simplify the basics for you. The following information is for anyone who comes in contact with another being. You can tailor it to your individual situation.

- Be accepting.

Focus on the positives and assist your children with the negatives. Don't expect perfection from them, or they will expect it from you. Remember they are often immature and frequently impulsive. Be patient with them.

- Be affectionate.

Hug them often and tell them you love them every day. Give them compliments and encourage them. Don't yell at them, hit them, call them names, or belittle them. Treat them gently and with respect. Treasure them.

- Be alert.

The world is full of dangers and temptations. As a parent or guardian, you are your children's protector. Watch over them and warn them.

Protect them without being paranoid. Most important, pray for them daily.

- Be approachable.

One of the biggest problems parents encounter is emotional distance from their children. Be close to them and spend quality time with them. Laugh with them, play with them, and truly enjoy them. Take them on walks, outings, and vacations. Focus and connect with them.

- Be assertive.

Pass on to your children the lessons you learned in life. Teach truth and honesty. Provide reasonable rules and consistent consequences when those rules are broken. Be strong. Give them security without being rigid, insensitive, abusive, angry, or exasperated.

- Be aware.

Study your children. They're wonderful creations. Listen to them, watch them, and ask them questions. Talk *with* them, not *to* them. Discover their likes and dislikes, their dreams and fears, and their strengths and weaknesses. Recognize how special and unique they are.

These easy steps will help to make a difference in others in a positive healthy manner. It's a lot of responsibility to be a positive figure in someone's life, but anyone can do this—just lead from your heart. You're going to be just fine.

People don't always need advice. Sometimes all they need is a hand to hold, an ear to listen, and a heart to understand them.

How to Handle Your Adult Children Moving Back In

Oh my, you just got off the phone with your adult child, who wants to move back in with you—along with his or her family—because something has suddenly changed in life. What do you do now? These situations can be exciting or a red flag. Your parental-instinct side tells you you're glad to help and would love having them all with you under one roof; it'll be fun. Your other side (or your mate), however, tells you it's a terrible idea, and it won't work.

What should you do when your adult children want to move back home?

First, let them know you'll be glad to talk about it, but do not give an immediate answer. Never follow a gut reaction and make a commitment on the spot. This will give you time to think of the entire picture and discuss the pros and cons with your other half (or just yourself).

The following are a few points to seriously consider, whether it's just one child or family members too:

Set up a time to sit down with all parties involved to discuss this potential move. If your child doesn't live in your city, set up a phone call. If your child has a mate, it's imperative that all adults be present on the phone or in person to ensure that everyone is on the same page.

Here are things to think about:

- Be in total agreement.

Before you take anyone into your home, agree with your mate (if you have one) to stand together on all decisions. If one partner is strongly opposed to the return of the adult child (with or without a family), the situation will never work.

- Establish control.

If your child comes back home, clearly spell out whose home it is.

When your kids show the first sign of bucking for control, you (and your mate, if applicable) must take quick action.

- Set a time frame for how long your child can stay.

Don't let anyone move in for an indefinite time.

- Assign jobs.

Do not start making their beds or doing their laundry or dishes. You already raised your family once; you don't need to do it a second time.

- Always keep your regular schedules and regular mealtimes.

If your new guests don't like what you've cooked or when you want to have meals, eat at separate times. Make it clear they can buy their own food, cook it, and clean up afterwards.

- They must be told this is your home, not a hotel.

Your new guests must know they're not to expect hotel services. In addition to establishing mealtimes and assigning cleanup, let them know you are not in charge of their business calls, their dry cleaning, or their change of linens.

- Financial contributions are a must.

If your child (and his or her family) stays for a week or two, your hospitality can be considered a very kind gift. If the established time frame is longer, however, ask them to share the expenses.

- Never let them criticize.

Let them know from the start that if they don't like your home, your agreement, your lifestyle, or your friends, they can leave.

- Their children are not your dumping ground.

When grandchildren move in, the grandparents sometimes use them to express feelings they won't share with the parents. The kids will tell their parents their own version or even repeat your version of what they heard. This will bring immediate ill feelings and trouble. Never talk about any concerns you have with their children. Instead talk to your own child and his or her mate (if applicable) immediately. Never let ill feelings or concerns fester; they are bound to come out, so communicate.

- Their children are not your responsibility.

Couples sometimes complain that their parents didn't always want to babysit so they could go out more. The parents may have said, "We didn't have these babies; you did. We love them, but we are not responsible for their care. When we babysit, it is a gift of love that we may offer for that time. It should never be expected."

If you've never been in this situation, you may think it wouldn't happen to you, but it *could*, and the above guidelines—though only the basics—will help. If you choose not to follow the guidelines, your relationship with your child likely will suffer. It's happened countless times. The situation will blow up out of proportion if you don't have it under control at the start. Don't allow your children's memories of you to be damaged by something that is totally preventable.

You cannot change what you refuse to confront from the start.

What Are You Leaving Behind
for Your Kids and Family?

I've been asked this question many times during my career as a medical professional: "Which would be better to leave behind for my kids and family—money or possessions?"

That's a complicated question. Think carefully about that. What would you like to leave behind for your kids or family? What would mean the most to them?

I've responded to that question over the years by asking, "What do you want them to have the most?"

The answers have been widely varied—money, cars, boats, assets, stocks, bonds, private collections, books, animals, vacations, time shares, the house, antiques, war medals, machinery, jewelry, gun collections, deeds, titles, technical equipment. It wasn't appropriate for me to give my opinion on what they should leave for their kids and family; the individual heart wants what it wants.

However, when those who had nothing to leave behind expressed great regret, I would give a simple response. I gave them the same answer that I gave my wonderful parents when they too asked me, "What can we leave behind for you that means the most to you?"

My answer was simply. "You already have. It's your qualities."

Qualities are not material or tangible; they're from within, part of you and your character, style, personality, and makeup. It's what makes you who you are.

I am forever grateful and truly proud that my parents instilled their qualities in me. I've mentioned these qualities previously, but they bear repeating:

- Honesty: always speak and live the truth.
- Responsibility: be trustworthy and dependable.
- Thoughtfulness: always think of others before yourself.
- Determination: stick with it until you get it.
- Confidentiality: never gossip or tell someone's secrets; keep your mouth shut.

- Punctuality: always be on time.
- Self-control: if you're under stress, always stay calm.
- Patience: be willing to wait; fight off irritability.
- Purity: reject anything that lowers your standards.
- Compassion: when others hurt, feel it with them.
- Diligence: always work hard, tough it out, and finish what you started.

Most important, these qualities come out naturally and consistently if you have them. You can never force them; they're "just there." Money cannot buy qualities like these; they're learned, and they're earned.

Leave something for others they can only get from you—your qualities.

Do You Show Your Kids Your Love?

Whether your "kids" are two-legged or four-legged, they're still your kids, and you should show them every day how much you love them. Here are a few examples of to show you love your kids:

o Take time with your kids.
o Set a good example for your kids.
o Give your kids ideals for living.
o Have a lot of activities planned with them.
o Discipline your kids; that is your responsibility.
o Teach them about God and spiritual understanding.

Don't let society raise your children; that is solely your responsibility. Be careful how you act and what you say in front of them because they are watching and listening. All they want to do is be like you, so look in the mirror and see if you need to make a few attitude adjustments on yourself.

Being a parent doesn't mean being related to someone by blood. It means loving someone unconditionally and with your whole heart.

CHAPTER 6

Mind-set

Mind-set is totally under your control; it refers to your beliefs, your intentions, and your actions. With a controlled mind-set and seeing your glass as "half full," you can achieve anything you set out to do. If you have a woe-is-me attitude, your glass will always be half empty. Consistently put into your mind what you want, believe you will get it, and act as if you already have it—that is very powerful. Your mind is what you feed it. If you feed your mind with garbage and negativity, this is what you will portray, but if you feed your mind with positive thoughts, a positive outlook is what you will portray.

Secrets to Genuine Growth

Do you ever think you don't need to learn anything new? Are you sure about that? Do you have all the information you need to live life and be successful? If so, you are in for a big surprise.

I actually heard two individuals make the following comments:

"I've been through school. I have a college degree and a graduate degree. I already know what I'm doing, I run a successful business. I have a good job. I'm practicing what I've learned and have more experience than you'll ever see in your lifetime."

"I learned all I need to know to get by. I went to the 'School of Hard Knocks' that taught me more than any program ever could. I'm fine."

Those two opinions might sound similar to something you've heard.

Can you see what is missing in these two comments? Neither one of has the main key—authentic genuine growth. They lack the internal growth within themselves. Book smarts and street smarts (hard knocks) alone will not help anyone to develop as a quality person.

Here are the secrets of genuine growth. See if you have any of these.

- Provide an example of commitment and integrity.
- Lead as you would like to be led.
- Constantly focus on the strengths of all with whom you come in contact.
- Have a passion for excellence.
- Savor the flavor of each passing moment.
- Infuse every thought and relationship with faith, hope, love, and gratitude.
- Ask, listen, and hear to determine the wants, needs, and possibilities of all with whom you come in contact.
- Follow a path of continual empowerment for yourself and others.
- Cultivate optimum physical, mental, and spiritual fitness.

You don't learn these things in schools, on the streets, or on your own without an open mind. These are the things that make you an outstanding person, an individual people look up to, a leader who has a passion for others more than himself or herself. These are what make a person into someone you would like to be. Develop these growth qualities—it's never too late.

But the secret is this: you have to believe these are within you and then consistently use them every moment of every day, without fail.

How wonderful that we needn't wait a single moment before starting to improve ourselves.

How to Become a Lifelong Learner

As children, our daily task was to learn as much as we could every day, to try new things and new experiences, and to test our nerves—when we're told no, we do it anyway. When we became young adults in college, we learned more academic or theory-based principles. During our adult years, we put into practice our theories and tested skills of what our earlier years and education taught us.

As we become more experienced, however, we try to learn something new every day. Sometimes that holds true; other days—well, not so much; life can get in the way.

Medical science has found that continuing to learn something new to challenge our minds is good for our brain cells and keeps them growing. The old saying "use it or lose it" holds true here—we need to continue to use our brain cells for stimulation and growth.

Continuing to learn things also provides continued growth within you. It's easy, doesn't cost anything, and is something you can and may be doing right now on your own. But the question is, are you doing it properly?

Here's how to become a lifelong learner:

- Start with your attitude. Lifelong learning begins with a heart that desires change, wisdom, and application.
- Ask questions that get below the surface. Learners ask probing questions. They possess a passionate curiosity and the longing to know, discover, and inquire about things.
- Join others. Collaborative learning in classes, small groups, or with friends and colleagues allows you to benefit from diverse perspectives and approaches. People are a gold mine of learning that can be tapped through conversations.
- Check out the other side. Take time to examine and understand another point of view openly, even if it radically contradicts yours. You may see things in a new light, or you may have your old convictions strengthened. Personal convictions that have never been tested can remain flimsy.

- Read broadly. Include diverse books, authors, and topics. Resist the temptation to read only those books that reinforce what you already believe or know. Include personal development books to help your self-growth to mature and stay positive about yourself.
- Keep a journal. Recording what you learn captures your growth in wisdom.
- Experiment. Try new approaches and ideas. Age does not affect your ability to learn. A ninety-year-old can learn to "surf the Net" as well as an eighteen-year-old.
- Apply what you know. Our depth of understanding is often directly related to our ability to apply what we've learned. Application of what we've learned takes knowledge from the brain to the heart.

Make it a point to learn something new every day. Make it a daily habit to learn and do something you've never done before.

Remember this: a day without learning new things is a day without growing.

> *You can't start the next chapter of your life if you keep rereading the last one.*

Do You Know How to Start a Conversation?

How do you start a conversation with your kids, with an adult, or with anyone, for that matter? Do you feel comfortable and confident starting conversations with others? Surprisingly, many people do not feel comfortable. They just hold back and wait for the other person to start talking. Some people genuinely have difficulty starting conversations with others.

For example, my oldest brother and I are very close, yet we both have this issue. We'll ride together in a car for miles before one of us starts a conversation after the small talk is completed. You might wonder how we can be close, care about one another, and be siblings, yet can't start a conversation with one another. My brother and I are both in professions in which we help others; we are constantly communicating, guiding, and teaching others with our knowledge and experience. We get along wonderfully, and we work well together and love each other. When it comes to just plain family conversation, though, we're at a loss for words.

When I had my accident, my brother rarely left my side. He protected me, spoke for me when I couldn't, and guided me when I needed help. He couldn't have done more for me. He's always been this way, and I've been that way for him. But until we land on a subject we're both passionate about, the silence can be deafening.

Experts often say it's a time of trust. When we are with someone we truly trust and with whom we feel totally comfortable, some of us have that time of trust, when saying nothing for a while is okay. We should not be offended by the silence.

My brother and I are both very shy, and we keep our personal issues and pain to ourselves. We don't gossip, we don't talk about or find fault with others just to talk, and we are not social butterflies. We have a lot of knowledge and experience to contribute, but otherwise, we are just *shy*. Many people have this issue; according to experts, it's very common, and there's nothing wrong with it.

I have collected conversation-starter suggestions for those who have trouble initiating a conversation. You can use most of these on adults or children because, let's face it, when your kids become a certain age, it's harder and harder to talk to them too. In addition, if you work in a profession where you seem to talk all day, when you get home you just don't want to talk anymore, so you let someone else start a conversation.

Try some of these conversation starters:

- What's your favorite food?
- What's your favorite song?
- What talent or skill do you wish you had?
- What was the best birthday present you ever received?
- What makes you laugh?
- If you could go anyplace in the world, where would you like to go for a vacation?
- If you had to move and could take only three things with you, what would you take?
- How would you describe the ideal father, mother, or family?
- What is something you can do well?
- What's your favorite color?
- What is your best friend really like?
- What's your favorite animal?
- How would you describe yourself to someone who does not know you?
- What is something that really bugs you; that is, what is your pet peeve?
- What kind of trophy would you like to win?
- Has there been a time when you felt particularly proud of yourself? What were you doing?
- What kind of store or business would you like to own and operate?
- If you received five thousand dollars as a gift, how would you spend it?
- What is your favorite room in the house? Why?
- What kind of a job do you want to have in five, ten, or twenty years?
- If you could receive anything in the world for your birthday, what would you like?
- What would you invent to make life better?

Are these weird questions to start a conversation? Not at all. For one thing, they'll help to start a conversation because they're not yes-or-no questions, and for another, these questions show the other person that you're interested in him or her. Try one of them the next time you don't know what to say. Who knows? You might learn something.

I have been given endless talents that I will begin to use today.

How to Keep Your Brain Healthy

Whether you're working, at home, in college, retired, traveling, out of work, or too down in the dumps to do anything, you need to be aware of and take care of your brain cells, just as you take care of other parts of your body. If you don't, they'll start to fail you—if they haven't already.

As I've mentioned, the old adage holds true: use it or lose it. But that phrase is particularly important when it comes to your brain cells. An infant's brain is an empty canvas to be filled with knowledge and learning. The brain cells are healthy and ready to be stimulated with information. As we age, however, that stimulation in the brain cells needs to continue, or the cells begin to slough off and die. Keep your brain cells working, nourishing them with information so they'll function properly every day. What can you do? Plenty of things!

- Write letters or poetry.
- Learn a foreign language.
- Play complex puzzles and games, like chess or Scrabble.
- Study music.
- Engage in thought-provoking discussions.
- Study history.
- Solve math problems without using a calculator.
- Sign up and learn a new sport.
- Study and memorize recipes, passwords, or scriptures.
- Read no less than an hour per day without interruptions.
- Learn how to play a musical instrument.
- Play cards.
- Learn to Knit, Needlepoint, Cross Stitch, Quilting Blankets.
- Learn Woodworking.
- Build Models.

Just as we learned daily as children, we must continue to learn daily as adults. Look for opportunities that will make you think on a regular basis. Find something that will challenge you. By doing these things for your brain cells, you might learn something.

Your mind is a terrible thing to waste.

How Well Do You Know Yourself?

To function well in life—to succeed, to grow, to love, to flourish, to thrive—you must know yourself. But how well do you *really* know yourself? If you don't know what you're made of, how you think, and your likes and dislikes, how will you ever know what your dreams, passions, and visions are? Simply put, you won't. Those around you already know you by how you project yourself, but for *you* to really know yourself, think about the following:

- What do you want most?
- What do you think about the most?
- How do you use your money and on what?
- What do you do with your leisure time?
- Whose company do you enjoy?
- Whom do you admire and why?
- What do you laugh at, or who makes you laugh?

These are the basics—your likes, thoughts, desires, enjoyment, and personal finances. If you don't know all of these answers, you need to dig deeper inside yourself to find out. In order to love yourself, which you must do before you can ever love anyone else, you first need to know about yourself. Only then will you be ready for your second step: believe in yourself. Once you believe in yourself, you can do anything.

You will never become who you want to be if you keep blaming everyone else for who you are now.

Share Your Smile with Someone Today

We all have busy minds. We walk around with our heads down, deep in our thoughts, on our phones. If our thoughts have the least bit of a bad day, or "I'm alone," or "I have to work," our facial expressions will show that unhappiness or tension or stress. The point I want to make is that no one smiles much anymore. The more I see people with their expressions that show their busy minds, the more I notice the lack of smiles.

On Valentine's Day, I tried an experiment when I encountered a sea of nonsmiling faces. I simply looked at an individual and, smiling, said, "Happy Valentine's Day!" In the split second that followed, what do you think happened? He (or she) smiled and spoke with such gratitude. From that point the person continued the conversation about their kids, spouse, friends, or whatever. Those three little words—happy Valentine's Day—and a smile just completely made their day. This is the same feeling people get on an ordinary day when you just smile and say hello to them. Today, share your smile and a pleasant greeting with someone.

Be kind and give smile to those you meet. You have no idea of the hell they may be experiencing.

How to Be More Creative in Your Thinking

Some people think that they know all there is to know about being creative and productive. Do you feel this way? I hope not, because if you do, then you aren't open-minded about learning new things. For us to be more creative or productive, we often just need something to trigger our thoughts.

I want to share some thoughts that might spark an idea—a word, a sentence, a visual—in your mind. You might even think of something you never thought of previously—and that will be even better because you'll have new thoughts. You might think you have enough to think about, and you may be right, but I'm referring to constructive, creative thoughts. Here's how to have more creativity in your thinking:

- Watch people. Go to town, to the lake, or to the mall. Sit on a bench, and observe people. Imagine what types of lives they lead.
- Wash dishes or mow the lawn. These are easy tasks, and both will give you a sense of accomplishment while you're thinking.
- Listen to music. Listen to whatever music sparks your imagination—classical, rock and roll, or something you've never heard before.
- Keep a journal. Write about your life and what's important to you. Revisit your old thoughts when you need new ideas.
- Exercise. Go for a run, shoot some basketball hoops, or do jumping jacks or anything that starts your blood pumping and keeps your mind sharp.
- Change your location. Find a new quiet place—a park, a beach, a library, or just a different room. Then let your mind wander. I call it "being still." When I'm just still, I find things come to me from my heart.
- Write it down right away. Write down ideas as soon as you think of them. Keep a paper and pen with you at all times—in the car, in your desk, by the TV, and on your nightstand.

- Do something poorly. If you're a perfectionist, don't be. Create something that isn't necessarily your best work but at least it gets the job done. Then go back later to fix it or redo it.
- Sleep on it. If nothing is working, your best bet may be to set it aside for now. Let you subconscious create overnight, and you'll have fresh ideas tomorrow.
- Brainstorm with a friend, coworker, an elderly adult, or even a young child. Talk with someone who looks at the world a little differently than you do. Chances are he or she will inspire a new approach.
- Pray and read the Bible or a personal development book. Putting life into spiritual perspective can take the pressure off and jump-start your creative juices.
- Freely write: Sit down at the computer or with pen or paper, and write whatever comes to mind. You will be surprised what comes out.

If you use any of the above suggestions with an open mind, it will trigger something in your thoughts to present something creative to you. Why do you need creative thinking? Learning something new or developing something creative is how you grow, how you expand, and how you succeed in life. Having new information, thoughts, and ideas is what makes you interesting, unique, and inspiring. Don't be tempted to sit in front of a box that plays games or presents shows or movies with content those creators want you to see. Be independent with learning and coming up with your own ideas, thoughts, and plans. Just remember you already have the information inside your mind. You only have to bring it out of you. Never force the thoughts; let them flow freely. Whatever you do, do it today, and most important—have fun.

Limitations live only in our minds, but if we use our imaginations, our possibilities become limitless.

Do You Believe in Yourself?

Regardless of your personal situation, it's important to believe in yourself. Believe you can get up. Believe you can do whatever it takes to get through your situation. Believe that you are a good, caring person.

Repeat the following sentence every day until you know them by heart: "I believe in myself. I believe I can get up. I believe I can do whatever it takes to get through this. I believe that I *am* a good, caring person."

Say it every day until you truly believe it. Those words need to be imbedded in your mind. If you don't believe in yourself, don't love yourself, or don't respect yourself, then don't expect anyone else to believe in you, love you, or respect you. The very first step to crawling back up after a devastating episode is to first believe in yourself.

You have to own that belief and own that trust, love, and respect in yourself. Then you have to wear it, showing your belief in yourself. ("I know this was rough, but I *will* get through this"). You have to understand you are the only one who can do this—just you. No one can come in to fix it and rescue you; that is *your* job. You can do it if you believe in yourself. The first step is always the hardest step, but you can take that first step and get through all of them if you continue to *believe*. If you still think no one believes in you, just know that I do.

> *"Believe you can, and you're halfway there."*
> —Theodore Roosevelt

What Life Lessons Have You Learned?

Everyone learns a lot throughout their lives. Good, bad, or indifferent, things were learned. Some of those lessons may be corny; some may have been sad. But I have to say bravo to you for continuing to learn, regardless of how hard or sweet it was.

I can pinpoint the significant lessons I've learned throughout my life and when I learned those life lessons:

- I learned at age five that I liked to play outside and be with nature because my mom cried when I brought her a bouquet of dandelions.
- I learned by age six that no matter how hard you try, you can't hide brussel sprouts in a glass of milk.
- I learned at about age eight that country folks seem nicer than city folks. When you wave to people in the country, they stop what they're doing and wave back.
- I learned when I was thirteen that if you want to cheer yourself up, you should try cheering someone else up.
- I learned at fourteen, although I never admitted it, that I was secretly glad my parents were strict with me.
- I learned at age twenty-two that my parents were my best friends. When I told them, they both cried and thanked me for telling them.
- I learned at age twenty-five that silent company can be more comforting, than words of advice.
- I learned at thirty-eight that if someone says something unkind and hurtful about me, I had to live in a way that no one would ever believe it.
- I learned at forty that regardless of your relationship with your parents (and mine was great with my parents), you miss them terribly after they die.
- I've learned the more someone has a sense of guilt, the more likely he or she will cast blame on someone else.

- I've learned that singing "Amazing Grace" to myself can lift my spirits.
- I've learned that you can tell a lot about a person by the way he or she handles a rainy day, lost luggage and tangled-up Christmas tree lights.
- I've learned that if you want to do something positive for your children, you should try to improve your marriage.
- I've learned that life sometimes gives you a second chance.
- I've learned that when you pursue happiness, it will elude you, but if you focus on the needs of others, happiness will find you.
- I've learned that whenever I have kindness in my heart while trying to decide on something, I usually make the right decision.
- I've learned that everyone can use a prayer.
- I've learned that even when I am having pain, I don't have to be one.
- I've learned that every day you should physically touch someone. People love human touch—a hug, pat on the shoulder, holding hands, or a friendly touch on their arm.
- I've learned I still have a lot to learn.

It's not so much what you learn or what you know;
it's what you do with what you know and have learned.

What Qualities Do You Have?

Going through rough times and struggling day by day, then losing the battle is one of the few times we really take a look at ourselves and ask, "How did this happen? How did I get here? What did I do wrong?" When we ask ourselves those questions, we further realize how lonely we feel. But what's one of the first things we do? We look around for someone to blame for our loss, our challenges, our hurt, our mess.

Blaming someone else is not the answer because he or she most likely had nothing to do with what happened to you. Shifting blame onto someone else is only avoiding the cause. Maybe you lack the qualities you must have to be the person you should be. Qualities make you a good person, and they come from within you. They are learned behaviors. Live every day by the qualities you have within you.

As I've previously mentioned in this book, some of the qualities by which you should live your life are honesty, responsibility, thoughtfulness, confidentiality, punctuality, self-control, determination, patience, purity, compassion, and diligence. These are qualities you should pass along to your children because these are qualities of a good, solid, successful, and positive person. Isn't this what we look for when choosing a friend, spouse, partner, or anyone else we what to be a part of our lives?

As a parent, you should already have these qualities. If you don't, then work on adopting these qualities as your own because your kids will they learn from you. As a person—whether you're a friend, spouse, partner, or coworker—you also should have these qualities. If you don't, you'll eventually find yourself alone.

Practice these qualities every day. What you do every day is what you will become.

Throughout your life and every day, remember your actions always speak louder than your words.

This Is Your Future

What are you going to do about your future? It's not complicated, it shouldn't be procrastinated, and you don't have to spend sixty years exhausting so you'll never enjoy it. If you are working night and day now to get to where you want to go when you retire, slow down a moment. We all need to plan, save, develop, and organize our lives, but whatever we're taught to plan for fifty or sixty years into the future is rather ambitious, don't you think?

We do not know what's going to happen one year, five years or even ten years from now, let alone a lifetime away. Consider the idea that who and where we will be in the next five years depends on three things:

- the people we meet and the relationships we make
- the books we read
- the choices we make

Reaching beyond five years does not allow us to build positive habits that will become automatic reflexes for us. We are creatures of influence. Our minds take in the influences—from people, books, and choices—and develop us along the way. Giving us five years at a time, instead of multiple decades, allows us to adjust to the changes in the world and things around us.

Choose today to live a transformed life!

Every single thing that has ever happened in your life prepares you for a moment that is yet to come.

How to Find the Right Person
as Your Listening Ear

We all know how to listen, don't we? Did you know, though, that listening to someone, actually means to "make an effort to pay close attention to what's being said"?

Now can say you really *listen*? Most of us think we are listening only because the other person is talking, and we aren't. Often, we're preoccupied with thinking about something else, and we think we know what the person is saying. If that's the case, we're terrible listeners. We may offer lots of comments, but we just don't listen very well.

How can you tell when someone is a terrible listener? It's when that person's responses have nothing to do with the topic of conversation. The person may deny that he or she wasn't listening, but the person's comments tell the whole story—he or she never heard a word you said.

How can you find someone who will really listen to what you're saying? How can you find the right person to be your "listening ear"? Look for someone who:

- has proven he or she can keep a confidence
- has proven he or she can respect your boundaries
- has earned your trust
- will give you perspective
- is wise and has more experience that you
- will pray for you sincerely
- values the commitment in a relationship
- will keep you accountable, without unjustly condemning you
- is of the same sex (or a married couple, if you prefer), to eliminate awkwardness.
- will not be negatively affected by your confidences

I've heard many people say, "I'm a good listener. You can talk to me." If you've made such an offer but you have issues, drama, or past feelings that are still unresolved, you are not ready to counsel others quite yet. In time, after you have resolved your personal issues, you may become a preferred listener because you went through it. Just don't offer to be a listening ear when you're in the middle of your own crisis and anxiety storm. You still need time yourself. It takes time and practice to be a good listener, one who makes an open, objective, unbiased, attentive effort. You should be able to hear and understand what someone is saying.

It's wonderful to have that "go-to" person on whom you can unload, that person who always seems to know how to listen. If you know someone you'd like for your sounding board but haven't had the courage to ask that person, go ahead and ask; you may be surprised.

Be sure that you listen to others, and see how they respond to what you're saying. Ask yourself, "Did she [or he] really hear what I said?" Then listen to the person's replies. You'll know soon enough if this person was listening.

It's better to be alone than to be in the company of someone who never listens.

How to Bury a Great Idea

Do you sometimes feel like you're banging your head against a wall? I am so blessed to be surrounded by awesome, caring, and giving people in my life, in my online business, at home, and as my friends and family. I hear so many offers for help, and we share many interesting conversations and great ideas. That, however, is not what I experienced in my past work life.

I love to hear new ideas because I learn new things and that often challenges me. Some people, however, can be a little stubborn when it comes to new ideas. The following are comments I actually heard almost daily at my previous workplace:

- We can't afford it.
- It will never work.
- We've never done it that way.
- We're doing fine without it.
- We're not ready for it.
- It's not our responsibility.
- We've always done it the other way.

Those comments won't let in new ideas, will they? The door is closed, the wall is up, and nothing's coming in.

If you don't want to be someone who buries new ideas, be flexible, and open your mind and heart to new ideas before you respond. Let your imagination see it as you listen carefully to another person's thoughts and ideas. Build your intellectual library with new thoughts and ideas.

Grow your mind, grow yourself, and see what you can learn. The beauty of everyone's being unique is that we all have different thoughts and ideas. Listen to others' ideas and share them. Explore and listen—— you may be surprised by what you learn.

> "A person who never made a mistake never tried anything new."
>
> —Albert Einstein

How to Find Someone to Listen

When you are going through challenges, it feels like everything is falling apart around you. Before this last big challenge brought you down, however, you were handling all things unknowingly. Now that you're down, you've given up. This, my friend, is a very normal feeling.

One thing that is key for you now is to find someone with whom you feel comfortable; someone you trust that you can talk to; someone who will just listen to you.

Right now, you're too overwhelmed to hear any advice; in fact, anything that anyone has so say to you will be more like noise. Your mind is full; what you need is to vent without restrictions, to get all that negative out, to unload all the stuff inside you that has put you down here.

Finding a good listening ear is hard, and there are a few things you need to recognize when you are considering someone to just listen.

Here's how to find someone to listen:

- Find someone you trust.
- Find someone who can keep a confidence. You don't want your mess talked about elsewhere.
- Find someone who will respect your boundaries.
- Find someone who will pray for you and with you.
- Find someone who will give you perspective only if you ask for it.
- Find someone who is wise and has more experience than you.
- Find someone who values commitment in marriage, friendship, partnership, or whatever you have in common.
- Find someone who will keep you accountable without unjustly condemning you. This is not the time for further punishment. You've gone through enough.
- Find someone of the same sex or a married/committed couple. You don't need to worry during this process about unknowingly giving mixed messages.

- Find someone who will not be negatively affected by your confidences. (What you have to say might be taken wrong, and you don't need to explain yourself.)
- A good listener is a gem. Be sure you are comfortable with that person and that he or she is comfortable with you.

Remember a listener is not a cure for what's going wrong with you right now. You're looking for someone with whom to have a quality conversation. A good listener is only there to help you vent and get all this negative out so you can start the process of healing.

> *People don't always need advice. Sometimes all they need is a hand to hold, an ear to listen, and a heart to understand them.*

Is No One Hearing You?

I'm going to talk about communication in an easy-to-remember way. After all, many of you are already stressed out, going through grief, wounded from a miserable day at work, or fighting with your spouse (or friends or kids or the mechanic or the pharmacy). I learned this in college in an advanced communications class and it's stuck with me because it's so easy to remember.

So, whatever is happening to you at this moment, *stop.* If you're still muttering "No one is listening to me," or "Who cares?," These thoughts must be stopped.

I want you to think of only one word: ladder. Again, think of *ladder.*

LADDER is an acronym that will help you remember very simply how to communicate with other people.

Look at the person speaking to you.
Ask questions.
Don't interrupt.
Don't change the subject.
Empathize.
Respond verbally and nonverbally.

Okay, get your own ladder out and use it!

Successful interactions first start with a willingness to listen.

When Are You Going to Take Responsibility?

Since we were children we have learned, experimented, explored, and tried new things. But when or how did we start to become responsible or have responsibility? Or are we just born that way? Did "responsibility" come with instructions? What does it mean to be responsible or to have responsibility?

Our parents paid taxes that provided us with the elementary school education that taught what big words meant. Back then, we learned that big words had only one correct definition (no matter how hard I tried to debate that issue).

So why are definitions of *responsible* and *responsibility* changed by some people to suit their needs? Regardless of your age, location, or education, responsible and having responsibility still means certain things you should keep in mind:

- Never spend your money before you have it.
- Never buy what you don't need just because it's cheaper today.
- Never put off until tomorrow what you can do today.
- Never trouble another for what you can do yourself.
- Pride costs you more than hunger, thirst, and cold.
- You never feel regret from having eaten too little.
- Nothing is troublesome that we do willingly.
- Take things by their smooth handle.
- When you're angry, count to ten before you speak; if you're very angry, count to one hundred while you walk it off.

Are these familiar phrases you grew up hearing? When did so many people stop practicing these? Why have so many people instead become irresponsible? If you are planning to or currently are trying to become successful in life or business, the definition hasn't changed for responsibility.

Since I've reminded you what not to do when being responsible, let's all start taking more responsibility for what we do. Life is incredibly short, be more responsible, accountable, agreeable and helpful.

Always be sure to taste your words, before you spit them out.

Did You Ever Receive Words of Wisdom?

After my devastating accident left me helpless—unable to care for myself, unable to use my dominant hand, arm, or leg because of multiple fractures, financially drained, and completely an emotional wreck—I knew I was not the same person anymore and believed I never would be again. I actually felt like a little no more than an infant.

While I was lying in the hospital for two weeks with complications, the activity going on around me was terrifying. My being a registered nurse from the ER made it even more terrifying because I knew too much. What I found was kind of weird, but to distract myself from the fear of the reality that had happened to me, I had conversations with myself going on in my head. Of course they weren't social conversations; they were more like telling myself, *Okay, you're going to be all right. You can do this. Everything will be back to normal as soon as you get out of here.*

Although I had those and many other internal conversations to reassure myself, things were not getting better. Still, I kept saying that when I got home they would be better. I was convincing myself that when I got to somewhere else, things would be back to normal.

Isn't that what everyone does—delay the accomplishment until the time is right, or the setting is right, or even when everything is organized? But that's not how accomplishments work. They do not just happen; you have to make them happen. You chip away at it every day to get closer and closer to your goal. Keep your focus on the end product, and don't lose faith. I watched a video made by a truly wonderful friend from New Zealand, in which she essentially said, "Just show up and put in the work every day. Don't give up on those down days."

Whatever you have to do to keep your mind focused and to keep reassuring yourself, do it. Just show up, and do it. Maybe it's a coach you who constantly drilled supportive, positive thoughts into your head, to the point you could hear them clearly in your mind, over and over.

Oddly enough, for me during my recovery, I suddenly remembered what my parents used to say to me when I was growing up. Then I actually began hearing myself talking to my patients everyday trying to motivate them to get up and just do it. Maybe for you it was your grandparents or an aunt who had the wisdom for you when growing up. I started to take those nuggets of wisdom that I remembered from my parents, from my nursing career and that is how I started to right the ship of my devastating condition. See if you remember being told any of these:

- You *can* do it.
- Your life can be anything you want it to be.
- Take things one day at a time.
- Manners matter in everything you do.
- Always treat others the way you would want to be treated.
- Always play fairly and honestly.
- Count all your blessings, not your troubles.
- Don't put limitations on yourself.
- It's never too late.
- Always put things back where and how you found them.
- Decisions are too important to leave to chance; be certain of your decision.
- You're never too old to do what's in your heart.
- Reach for the stars and grab them; don't just look at them.
- Always clean up after yourself.
- Nothing wastes more time and energy than worrying.
- The longer you carry a problem around, the heavier it gets.
- Say "I'm sorry" when you've hurt someone, and mean it.
- Even a little love goes a long way.
- A solid friendship is always a good investment.
- Never take things too seriously.
- Always love and believe in yourself, or nobody else will.
- It's always better to give than to receive.
- Don't start something you don't believe you can finish.

With all my injuries, I knew I had to start using these parental words of wisdom, Why? Because when I finally got home and was alone, I knew my recovery was up to me alone. The first thing I had to do was to get my mind and my thoughts straight and think positively.

Whatever you are going through—a loss, illness, injury, separation, divorce, financial loss—get your mind and your thoughts straight and more importantly, get your thoughts POSITIVE.

It's very easy to slide into giving up—trust me; I know—but it's also a deadly outcome for yourself. I found myself sliding down a black hole of doom after I was released from the hospital to home. I had no idea how injured I really was until I found out I could not care for myself, at all. Even the most basic necessities I could not do for myself. I was terrified and that black hole was continuing to close in. The shear fear of what was happening to me kept me frozen in time until I almost gave up. It wasn't until that one day I heard the short videos about strength, positive thoughts, pushing yourself, show up, try … then after a few days it hit me; that's the positive thoughts my parents raised me with, that's what I use to say to the patients I cared for, I need to do this.

Find something to give yourself drive. "Show up" every day, no matter what, and do it. When you feel the worst and the most down, that's when you need to show up and do it the most. Don't stop pushing yourself forward. Believe in yourself, and believe in and visualize your goal. Just show up!

You are braver than you believe, stronger than you seem & smarter than you think

"Stop Telling Me to Be Positive!"

Have you had those times when absolutely nothing was going right; when friends and family were trying to help and were encouraging you to "just think positive"?

Ugh!

Well, they were right. The issue causing your frustration, however, might be a little too fresh and raw at the moment. If so, now is not a good time to hear that encouragement (and if you're the one saying it, it's a terrible time to encourage that).

Why do people do that when you're furious and feeling down? Those who want to help use that "Just think positive" phrase because that's what they've been told in the past. They don't know what else to do or say, so they tell you to think positive. Is it wrong to tell someone to think positive, to encourage someone through a hard time? Isn't that what we're supposed to do?

Well, yes and no, but your timing may really stink.

Not all people who have gone through a negative incident are qualified to counsel and advise others of what to do. I'm saying that if you experienced a hardship in the past, had negative encounters, or were psychologically affected, you might not be the one to counsel someone else on his or her problems, thoughts, or issues. Your best intentions to help someone actually may cause more harm than good.

There are areas, however, with which you can help. I have known people who were going through their own hell, yet they somehow managed themselves, hour to hour, day to day, while they actively were going through their issues. They would turn around, however, and actively counsel other people with whatever their issues were. They sometimes took the information they were given for their own issues or that they read and immediately turned it around, using it to counsel others. Their theory was that they felt it was helping them to work through their own issues by helping others. Their intent to help was in the right place and the information they shared was good. Neither, however, was meant as a fix-all for anyone's issue. Those talks or readings they received were meant for their own individual issues.

It's wonderful to help others and to help yourself too, but remember you must have your own issues resolved before you "hang out your shingle" and counsel others. If you're still going through any of your own stuff, you are far from the point of being ready to guide others.

It takes a lot of time to heal those wounds, and if they're still raw, you will feel the effects from them. Wounds may not be healed because you've spent years pushing your issues down and trying to bury them. Regardless, you aren't ready to help others until you practice the helpful suggestions yourself.

The best way you can help others is by doing the following:

- Suggest a book that you found useful.
- Suggest an audio tape of a useful story.
- Refer them to a speaker who was of help to you.
- Refer them to a professional who has done a lot of counseling, who has experience with counseling patients, or to the one who helped you.
- Refer them to an author who talks on that subject.
- Suggest a helpful device or object that you used for the same issue.
- Suggest a particular store where they can find something they need.
- Refer them to an organization for support with their issues.
- Suggest a brochure or materials that will give them further information.
- The best way you can help yourself is to:
- Continue to practice the information that was given to you in confidence for your own issues.
- Continue to read your personal development books.
- Continue to listen to your audio tapes.
- Continue to follow authors and speakers who give you the confidence affirmations you need.
- Tell your story: "This is what happened to me."

A negative mind, will never give you a positive life

How to Handle Others When You Felt So Bad and Down Yourself

How you can best help everyone, including yourself?

Telling your story lets others relate and see that they are not alone in their issues.

Telling your story lets people identify with and feel empowered that they were not alone in the pain, fear, sorrow, or horrific experience.

Telling your story gives others hope—if you went through it, there is a light at the end of the tunnel of what they thought was only darkness.

Telling your story lets them know there can be a positive outcome of something they cannot see.

In telling your story, they can see it is worth trying to believe again.

You have personally experienced information that is real, raw, and amazing. The best part is that you survived it; you lived it. So if you really want to help someone, just tell your own story. Your story is the most powerful, helpful, gracious thing you can do for someone else. Let others see that you got through it. Listen to the words as you read your own story. Realize that the person in that story—your story—is a survivor! Listen to the details of hell that person went through. See how that story—your story—brought you to where you are today. Watch how your story alone is helping others. The response may be immediate or it might be delayed, but the response from your listeners or readers will be moving.

If you're currently feeling the aftereffects or continue to have the issues every day, it's okay just tell your own story. We are all works in progress. We are all learning. We are all recovering from something, somewhere, somehow, for whatever reason.

Stay away from counseling, advising or getting involved with others' recovery.

Just tell your story. Period. There are others who are going through what you are and they can relate. Hearing others have gone through it too, helps them to work through theirs.

Take pride in how far you've come. Have faith in how far you can go.

"I've Always Done Things This Way!"—How to Develop a Healthy Internal Growth

Doing something the same way for so long is not a good practice, nor is it healthy. It's time for taking inventory within yourself. You can't keep faking your way through your days when you feel like that. In order for you to start the process of growing— internally, emotionally, and physically—from learning new things, you need to do a lot of cleaning out within yourself.

After all the hurt, stress, anger, loss, challenges, and despair you have been through, you first must reprogram your thoughts.

Then you must learn new things in order to grow.

Impossible? Not at all, but you must be willing to learn new things, have an open mind, and accept the fact that you do not know everything. Start thinking differently than you have been—your current thinking got you to the point where you are now, the stagnant point where you do all the same things in the same way, over and over. You haven't been growing internally at all. You are just on autopilot!

Try some of these new things, for example:

- Develop a constant focus on the strengths of all that you come in contact with.
- Commit to physical, mental, and spiritual fitness daily.
- Have a passion for excellence, for doing things right instead of just getting by.
- Ask, listen, and hear.

In order to determine the wants, needs, and possibilities of others, you have to ask, listen, and understand.

- Provide a positive example of commitment and integrity with honesty.
- Follow a path of continual investment in yourself and in others.
- Lead others as you would like to be led.

- Savor each passing moment. You've no doubt heard the phrase, "Stop and smell the roses." *Savor your moments* is the same thing.
- Inject every thought and relationship with gratitude, love, hope, and even faith.
- Be open to change, and realize how healthy it is for you and your own mind.
- Understand that being stagnant will never allow you to grow and learn how things could be.
- Remember this is your life, and living is about learning and experiencing all you can.

Beautiful things happen when you open your mind to new things.

I Just Can't Do It Today

I've heard the comment, "I can't do this." Maybe you feel that way. Many of us have blurted that out a time or two. After my surgeries following my accident (and I had several), I have to admit I was tempted to talk negative. But I stayed strong.

I was *so* close to saying those four dirty words: "I can't do this." Instead, I said, "You can do this, one step at a time."

- Mind-set is a daily activity, always.
- Watch your thoughts; they become words.
- Watch your words; they become actions.
- Watch your actions; they become habits.
- Watch your habits; they become character.
- Watch your character, it becomes your destiny.

Turn your cannots into cans, & turn your dreams into plans.

How Do You Handle Failure?

I love golf. I love being out there, playing every hole. I love the scent of being outside, the sounds of the birds, and the challenge of playing. Of course, I'm not on the LPGA. I'm not a zero handicap. I'm not even on the wannabe tour. I just love to play golf and challenge myself.

In sports, as in life, business, and relationships, there are losses. Not everyone can win while in competition, but the strongest winners are those with the superior skills, character, and maturity, among others qualities.

I watched an LPGA (Ladies Professional Golf Association) tournament, which is a major tournament and the women's equal to the men's PGA (Professional Golf Association) Masters Tournament. Competition, whether between two individuals or hundreds of others, will have only one who succeeds as the winner. Whether it's an organized sporting event or a competitive debate, the circumstances are the same—only one person or team will prevail as the winner.

We learn about winning as children. "I'll race you to the tree"; "I can eat more hot dogs than you"—whatever the situation, it works the same. In business, staff members try to outdo each other to complete the task, to impress their boss, and to align themselves for more points or a promotion. Regardless of the competition, winning and losing have something in common—how the win or loss is handled by that particular person. While watching this LPGA tournament, I couldn't help thinking how very similar the pressure, stress, desperation, and will to win and succeed is to everything we handle in our daily challenges.

The impressions we make on others, the observations, and the visible body language speak volumes louder than the words we speak about the actual task or situation at hand. While I was watching the results and feedback about who won that golf tournament, it was completely overshadowed by the impression the loser's body language gave to thousands of viewers and the media. She spoke not a word about the loss or the activities during the three-hole playoffs, nor did she say a single negative word about her competitor during the post-tournament interview.

The viewers, however, surely must have perceived her quiet, straight-faced, focused manner and that she kept to herself, not engaging with the fans on the course during play as being negative. It's not so much the words you speak that others perceive as negative as that your actions can leave an impression on others. This player who lost did nothing, verbally or physically, to warrant the negative reviews, but others felt that her body language gave the wrong message. Is that right or fair? No, but nothing in life is fair. People always will feel they have the right to judge you. I was happy, however, with the skills of the individual who won the tournament. I was impressed with her maturity and class in how she handled the win; she was sensitive and respectful of the emotions and skill of her competitor.

Here's what you should keep in mind about failure in case you ever have an issue that doesn't go your way:

- To fail is not the same as being a failure. You may have many failings, yet be far from a failure.
- To fail is not the disgrace some think it is. To err is to do nothing more than be a part of the reality of life.
- Failure is only a temporary setback. Failure is never the final chapter in the book of your life—unless you give up and quit.
- Nothing worthwhile is ever achieved without running the risk of failure. When you risk everything to achieve what you want, it's far from being a failure.
- Failure is a natural preparation for success. Success can be difficult to maintain unless you continue to work at it daily.
- Every failing brings the possibility of something greater. You have to work at finding the seeds that will turn your failures into your successful growth.
- What you do with failure in your life is up to you. Failure can be a blessing or a curse, depending on how you react or respond to it.
- Failures are opportunities to learn how to do it better next time by recognizing the pitfalls and how to avoid them. Learn all you can from them.

No one really "fails." You're not a failure; you're not a loser; you're not anything but someone who tried to do his or her best at the time. In competition, there is always a winner and a loser. In life, however, everyone is a winner, and there are no losers. Anyone who makes an attempt to achieve something is a winner because that person made the effort to try and not give up. You succeed when you participate in life. You're a winner because you show up and give it your best.

Don't wear your negative results in your body language. Posture yourself as the winner that you are, not what the scoreboard has labeled you to be. Be proud of your participation and your attempt, and wear it proudly because in the competition of life, you'll always be a winner and successful.

Take pride in how far you've come. Have faith in how far you can go.

Lifting Your Mood

I recently had a wake-up call that started with the usual: Hi. How are you?" but quickly shifted to the caller saying, "I'm in such a bad mood." The rest of the conversation was a series of details about how miserable her weekend was, which overflowed into the days that followed.

After the first ten minutes, I had to say, "Stop!"

Some of you may be shocked or feel that was negative of me to stop the person from talking and maybe also thinking I wasn't listening to them. Actually, I was listening to what they were saying, but there comes a point when repeating and repeating the same words, the same issues or negative thoughts, will only impregnate into your subconscious, causing you to believe only what you consistently repeat.

Your subconscious mind is a kind of creative mechanism that is very powerful and even more powerful than your conscious mind. The subconscious – creative mechanism in fact forms and shapes us by projecting us into who we are as a person When you feel negatively about yourself all the time, for example; I'm so fat, I am so broke, I am so tied, I am such a loser, no one wants to be around me, I don't know how to do anything, I hate myself, I hate my job … all of that negative reflection of yourself, that you are carrying around is being submitted directly into your brain, subconsciously. Therefore, if you continue to tell yourself how awful you feel or how much of a "bad mood" you're in, I cannot do this, etc., your subconscious has been fertilized with all the negative and in turn all of that negativity is projecting outward to everyone.

Now, your subconscious-creative mechanism in your brain is carrying around all that negative bad feelings and projection of yourself towards others also: bad-mood, woe-is-me, I-hate-my-life, I-hate-my-job, the negative talk, all of the time. In turn, because the subconscious mind is the storage house for your self-image and how you really feel, others around you can 'feel' your negative projection before you even speak a word, that is how powerful your subconscious mind is. The subconscious mind information is the hardest to ever erase.

Just remember, what you put in and feed your mind with, is always kept in your subconscious and that is what you hang onto.

Tips to Lift Your Mood:

- Stop being negative. Turn negative thoughts and words into positive. It happened, let it go, and move on.
- Stop gossiping. Talking about someone else to make yourself feel better is negative. Gossip is not truth; it's someone's interpretation of truth.
- Say no to the negatives in your thinking. Say no to overloading yourself with things to keep you mind busy. It already is busy.
- Give up giving up. Give up the talk of a bad day and "woe is me," and think about the reasons why you are fortunate in your life.
- Let go of grudges. It's only eating away at you and increasing your stress level. Forgive and relieve your subconscious mind.
- Stop putting yourself down. Speak about yourself only positively, and say thank you to compliments. Believe you are good, and your subconscious will believe.
- Stop taking yourself so seriously. Think of a joke that made you laugh. Laughing is healthy for your heart and puts things in proper perspective.
- Stop worrying about what others think. Who cares? Focus on being a good person and helping others. That will strengthen your self-esteem.

Life is 10 percent what happens to you and 90 percent how you react to it.

Taking One Day at a Time

Are your Mondays mood-influenced? Mondays truly get a bad rap, and Fridays get all the love. We've heard the whining, the complaining, the ugly labels, and the bad hype about Mondays. Nothing surprises us anymore about people's negative feelings about Mondays.

How about the Monday after the Super Bowl? If you're a fan of the losing team, it's going to be a long, tough day, but if you're a fan of the winning team, that Monday is awesome. Suddenly, Monday isn't the day of the week that everyone dreads and dislikes.

Let's get real; the day of the week has nothing to do with your mood—or does it? Studies have indicated that yes, it does have everything to do with it for a lot of people. After all, the Carpenters even wrote a song about it, "Rainy Days and Mondays," so it must be true! Anecdotal studies have shown how awful Mondays are, and *US News & World Report* completed a poll, asking, "Do rainy days, winter days, or Mondays make you feel depressed?" Eighty-seven percent of those polled answered yes; 13 percent answered no, but since the question covered rainy days and winter days as well as Mondays, the poll couldn't pinpoint Mondays.

So, is Monday really the worst day?

The *New York Times* once wrote, "There is strong evidence that we hate Monday because we are supposed to hate Monday." It further claimed, "Several studies show that Monday is not the worst day of the week and only rates marginally less exciting than Fridays for most people." Of course, the media is not infallible. The only reason I knew about that article was because the Academy of Emergency Medicine was doing their own study about on which day of the week there were more traumatic incidents that increased the average number of patient visits in the emergency rooms. That study's results were inconclusive, and it was thrown out.

Could we say that everyone dislikes Monday? No, that's not true at all. In fact, a few weeks ago, I met a wonderful new friend, a successful entrepreneur from New Zealand, and she happens to adore Mondays because she gets to "recharge" on Mondays. There is actually a lot of truth to my friend's comment about Mondays because many things can be credited just to the fact that it *is* Monday. For example:

- Start out fresh. On Mondays, take advantage of a fresh start at the beginning of the week, and change your boring, usual to-do list, and make it more appealing and fun. By Friday, you will feel much better when you see you've accomplished a more energized list.

- Give yourself a second chance. You have a fresh start to the week, a chance to do better or perform better than you did last week. If you're the grumpy one on Mondays, start Monday by leaving all the negative outside. Just because you're grumpy, there is no reason to bring everyone else down. Remember that it's not just your words that show negativity; your actions also bleed negativity. Your negative mood will have a domino effect on everyone around you in less than fifteen minutes within your whole department at work. Negativity is very contagious and fast spreading and is a sure-fire way to kill anyone's positive mood. Just image being on the receiving end of your grumpy mood. No one likes walking on eggshells around one person who is grumpy, so get over yourself. It's not fun to be around you when you are grumpy.

- Stop being a drag. Look at Mondays as being about new opportunities, second chances, new responsibilities, being useful, trying new things (like your attitude), and being more mature once you keep the positive outlook going. This is your chance to stop being negative and be positive for the rest of the day, at home and at work. Be honest and dig deep within yourself. Figure out what makes you such a negative drain and behave more positively with others.

I challenge you to be consistent and leave your negative moods in the garbage on Monday and then on Tuesday and for the rest of the week. Over the weekend, look back and remember how you and everyone around you felt.

Stop listening to the negative news on the radio and television. Stop reading the negative news in the paper, and stop complaining! Turn on upbeat, positive music, and sing along in your car, in the house, or at the office. Stop being offensive by swearing all the time, and use your fingers for tapping to the music. Smile at people, open doors for others, and don't be in a rush to beat someone to the stop light.

Think about this: take an honest look at who is observing your negative and offensive behavior—your kids, spouse, friends, parents, coworkers, pets. If you're projecting your negativity on these people, they don't deserve to be treated like that. It's disrespectful, selfish, and energy-draining for them. How you do one thing is how you do everything--it becomes what you're known for.

So if you *think* you are going to have a terrible day, then that is exactly what will happen. Your attitude and thoughts first thing in the morning, just like on Monday, will determine the rest of the day and the rest of the week.

You also might try making a few tweaks to your diet. Include salads, eggs, green tea, apples, cinnamon, and even a little chocolate, all of which are natural ways to boost your mood and energy. You should, however, avoid too much caffeine or sugar. While you may feel an immediate energy boost, the crash later may make the caffeine and sugar a very bad choice.

Make Mondays a fresh start, a day to recharge yourself, and an opportunity to get a second chance to improve over last week. If last week was great, then make this week even better. But start today fresh and new because today *is* the first day of the rest of your life.

Today, be the badass person you were too lazy to be yesterday

How You Start Your Day Can Change Everything

How do you start your day? How does your day begin the moment you open your eyes? For many of us, an alarm clock buzzes, startling us out of maybe a wonderful dream. For others, the alarm may be music, which also may be startling if the volume is high enough. In college I had a very hard time getting up, so I had *four* large, Big Ben, loud-ringing alarm clocks that I placed strategically around the room, set five minutes apart and far enough away so I couldn't reach any of them. That meant I had to get up and walk to them to shut them off. Without fail, however, I seemed to wind up back in the warm bed and of course fell back to sleep. I lived in an apartment off campus, my bedroom had no heat, so I had what became my back-up plan to get me up and start my day on a more positive note.

This method happened by chance, but it worked for me. For some unknown reason, only after my fourth alarm clock went off and if I crawled back to bed, my cat, who had free rein of the apartment, went into action. She, my cat Kelli, would get on the bed, stand on my chest, pat me with her paws on my cheeks, and give my nose a lick! I always thought that was very sweet. For all the mornings since my college years, I have been awakened by whoever gets to me first: the gentle paws of the dogs on the side of the bed or the feisty cats.

When and how you start your day is very important because it sets the tone for the rest of your day. Your state of mind in the first few minutes after you wake up has a large influence on how your day will be. But first of all, you have to fight off the negative thoughts about the day's activities. Don't wake up thinking, *Oh man, I don't want to go to work,* or *Oh, it's too cold out there,* or *I'm already late. So what?* or *I hate my job.* All that negative puts you into a negative mind-set, and your whole day will reflect only negativity. Is that what being given a life is supposed to be like—always negative?

Do not start a new day feeling all the negatives you felt before you went to bed. Do not start your day with the hatred of yesterday. Every morning we wake up is the first day of the rest of our lives—believe it, think it, feel it, and embrace it because this new day is your new start, your new chapter in your life, your chance to change your attitude about everything that made you become negative. Do it, feel it, live it, and try on the feeling of looking at something in a positive way. Take this new positive feeling for a test drive, and see how it feels to smile at things that used to tick you off. Say hello to people you don't care for, open the door for others, and listen as they say thank you. Wave hi to the crossing guard who is standing out in the cold to protect your children as they cross the street. Offer to carry something that is weighing another person down.

Listen to what happens when you give a hand to others out of kindness, or give someone a smile when you see he or she looks angry. The appreciation you hear from others by holding the door, smiling at an elderly person, or saying hello to someone you don't like will surprise you. You usually might not hear the sound of appreciation—someone telling you thank you—so it may sound a bit foreign to you. Some people might feel strange when they hear you say hello or see you holding a door or waving to them because they'd become used to your negativity.

Just smiling at someone can change them for that moment. Just saying hi to others, whether you know them or not, makes them smile inside, and it releases a chemical in their brains that is soothing and calming. When you smile at a stranger who happens to be alone, you have no idea how that might have made the person's day—it might have been the first nice greeting he or she had all day. That person you held the door for might have been too weak to open that door himself, and the simple act of kindness helped to encourage him.

When you feel negative, you act and sound negative to everyone who sees you, hears you, and is around you. Negative projects negative, and others know (even your pets); everyone knows. Negative people can be picked out of a crowd; why would anyone want to be around someone who is negative all the time? That projection of negative energy is draining, not just to the negative person but to everyone around him or her. It's honestly exhausting to be around negative people because negativity acts as a vacuum, and it sucks all the joy out of everyone else—it's like poking a hole in a balloon.

When you feel positive, you encourage and lift up others who see and hear you. Positive projects positive, and others know (even the pets) and feel your positive energy. Positive people smile a lot, automatically do kind things for others, and feel happy to help others. Being positive is a feeling that others want to be around, and it becomes contagious. Those who come around you can't help but feel compelled to project positive energy themselves because it makes them happy too. Others feel charged around a positive person; they feel ambitious, lighter, and work goes by quicker. Amazingly, everyone gets along.

You have a choice every day when you wake up and start your day— to be negative and project toxic energy to everyone else, or to be positive and project the positive energy that becomes contagious. I am going to leave you with one of my favorite quotes. Think about what the message is saying:

Be kind. Everyone you meet is fighting a battle you know nothing about.

What Successful People Know about Adversity

I can't ...
It won't work ...
I don't have time ...
I don't know how ...
It will never work ...
I hate doing something new ...

What do all of these phrases have in common? Have you ever used any of these phrases?

Their one common denominator is that they are all negative words that will stop people in their tracks. Can't, won't, don't, hate, never—these words give a tense feeling. Can, will, make, always, love, try, give—these words feel brighter and happier. If people use the tense words on a daily basis, their subconscious thoughts tend to be negative. On the other hand, if a they use the happier words, their subconscious thoughts tend to be more positive.

Words become part of who you are, and if you use negative words day after day, in time your subconscious believes everything you face is a negative, and therefore you will not succeed. You will become weak, and you will live every day projecting negativity because it has become a learned behavior. When you use positive words day after day, however, in time your subconscious believes everything you face is a positive, and therefore you will not only succeed, but you expect to succeed. Responding in a positive way, you also project qualities of strength, character, and courage from deep inside you because it has become a learned behavior.

Negativity is a killer of the spirit in life, and negativity is a killer of the challenges in business. Negative people get very easily caught up in a life of self-pity, the "why me?" and the unfairness of life. By being negative, we miss the opportunities around us for growth and wisdom that are part of adversity. However, when we're positive, we allow ourselves to think much more clearly and deal with the hurdles that stand in our way.

Successful business entrepreneurs realize adversities (hardships, misfortunes) are part of life and deal with them in a positive manner, again from learned behavior. Those with the biggest challenges seem to respond with enormous wisdom, will, strength, character, and courage that comes from the positive subconscious. Successful people learn from the difficulties they face and find the strength to overcome them. Successful business entrepreneurs take each adversity as a learning challenge, and their perseverance emerges from deep inside them. Successful individuals believe in themselves; they overcome the negativity by conditioning their minds with certainty. Successful people's belief and certainty is a mind-set they have developed that produces positive constructive results on a daily basis. They know and believe in their minds they have the results they need for their success.

Mind-set is the very basis on which Tony Robbins has lectured and taught entrepreneurs for years. His famous formula for success is actually very simple: absolute belief leads to massive potential, which leads to massive action, which leads to massive results—and this circle of success continues over and over, developing certainty in your mind.

So change your mind-set. Turn your "I can'ts" into "I cans," and your dreams into your plans. If you do not *actively* change a negative outlook and what you are putting in your mind and thinking every moment, every hour and every day, you will never change your negative mind-set. Even the best in the business, like Tony Robbins, will tell you to "create a ritual daily that changes and trains your mind." If your thoughts are about starting a business for yourself, he says, "you must first find the *why*." You must dig deep and discover why you want to start a new business. Is it because you are tired of working hard to make someone else rich at your expense? Is it because you want to live the lifestyle you've always dreamed of? Is it because you want to buy a new home or new car or travel the world with your kids and spouse? Or is it to keep yourself out of debt?

We all have our own reasons for changing our lives and even getting into a new business. Whatever your reason is, you must find it, visualize it, and take massive action to reach your results with a positive mind-set.

Create a ritual daily that changes and trains your mind
– Tony Robbins

How Do You Develop Character

Where does character come from? Everyone has his or her own character, style, and make-up. We are who we are. The old saying that no two people are alike would fit regarding someone's character. Genetically, we are who we are because of what we were born with. But who are you, really? What makes who we are?

Outside of the physical body, we are all very different. We are different from one another because of our individual character. *Character* refers to our morals, integrity, ethical structure, attributes, and our overall reputation. It's what makes us unique and is how we're recognized or remembered. How do you develop character? What does character look like?

Look at the people you already know. What makes one person different from another or from you, other than physical appearance and the clothes he or she wears? How does one stand out, different from others?

Here are the basic qualities of people with character:

- They tell the truth.
- They don't gossip.
- They do what is right.
- They walk with integrity.
- They don't mistreat people.
- They side with those who are right.
- They keep their word.
- They don't take advantage of people for financial gain.
- They lend money to those in need without interest.

How do you look when you have character? From deep inside, you carry yourself with of the qualities listed above, and you subconsciously project them. It's your posture, your words, your integrity, your morals, your attributes, and your reputation.

"You become what you believe."

—Oprah Winfrey

Who Is Your Hero?

Do you have a hero? Did you have one as a child? Most kids do—a superstar athlete, singer, action figure, movie actor, television series star, musical superstars, or maybe their parents.

What really is a hero? The basic definition is, "someone who is noted for his or her special or exceptional achievements." As children, we kept our heroes vividly in our minds throughout the day and night. We wanted to be like them, to have their skills and talent. Today, thanks to merchandising, we can "wear" our heroes with pride on clothing and gear. You name it, and your hero's name or picture is on it.

Maybe you're struggling to get by right now, and you can't afford memorabilia items; they're expensive. That's okay. You don't need to buy anything because you can become someone else's new hero.

Most of us had at least one hero when we were growing up because it gave us a sort of escape from reality to an imaginary world or life—an adventure somewhere else for a while. Who is the most memorable hero who will live in your heart forever? Is it the superhero conquering the bad guys? Is it the sports superstar who made the winning shot, putt, goal, homerun, or point? Is it the artist with the spectacular performance or song?

The real hero is the individual who spends time with you, the one you can do fun things with and not realize you learned something special. Who can be a hero? Anyone who cares.

Kids today desperately need a hero who:

- listens with both ears and eye contact, even if it means getting down on one knee
- laughs until his or her belly hurts and tears flow, while secretly creating deep friendships and memories that last a lifetime.
- plays catch, loves tea parties, plays tag, or even wrestles because the heart of a child is right there, and the person sets out to capture it before it's gone
- makes mistakes but considers them to be wonderful opportunities to learn

- makes time for a child's soccer, baseball, or basketball game; a school play; or ballet, tap, or gymnastics class because it's a priority to the child
- loves at all times because love is a gift that's freely given and not a reward for service well done
- hears about those in need and is flexible enough to say, "Let's do something to help right now," and then gives generously of his or her time and kindness
- gives the credit to others and empowers those he or she touches to succeed in everything they do
- models love as action, commitment, and truth, even when it hurts, because he or she believes God can work miracles in even the hardest heart

A hero is not about money, ranking, popularity, stature, or connections. A true hero gives of himself or herself unconditionally and consistently.

So, do you have a hero? For me, it was always my Dad, he was my hero. It was never about money, ranking, connections or anything to do with medals. My Dad was my hero because of his heart, he cared, he was patient and he was giving. My Dad made time for me to learn things that were beyond my years, not with books, not with numbers or things. My Dad taught me how to use my hands to accomplish tasks, to make and build things, to fix things, to finish things. My Dad taught me it was more practical to use common sense rather than 'things' to make something work and complete a task. In later years when I asked my Dad why he had always taught me hands on skills, he looked at me and said, "I want you to always know how to take care of yourself without the needs of others". Ironically that was at the time in my life I was beginning to regret not spending enough time along side my Mom to learn more about cooking. Although, my Mom had already told me; "don't worry about cooking Linda, you can always read a recipe, your Dad is trying to teach you Life Skills, so just concentrate on that". I not only concentrated on that, I thoroughly enjoyed that and felt incredibly grateful for all the skills I have been given.

Go and thank your hero for caring enough about you that they shared themselves with you. Those are the things that have shaped you into who you are today.

> *"People will forget what you said, people will forget what you did, but people will never forget how you made them feel."*
>
> —Maya Angelou

What in the World Do We Need?

I made a dreaded mistake recently. I decided to get caught up on what was going on in the world, so I thought it would be a good idea to watch the news.

My reaction? What has happened to everyone? What trend is drastically changing all the people of this world? Everything's in a free-fall everywhere.

When you don't watch or read the news regularly, you are away from all the negative "stuff" going on everywhere—murders, rapes, deaths, story after story. I hadn't been living under a rock; I'd been living my life, working hard every day to get myself back after my accident. I'd been consciously giving myself positive thoughts and affirmations to give me the fuel I needed to get back up. But after watching the news report, I was grateful (and still am) that I'd taken the positive route. If I'd chosen hateful, negative thinking like I heard on the news, I'd be dead by now.

It made me wonder what's happened to people's morals, honesty, and character. I think folks have a lot of work to do on themselves. Watching the news made me think: why is there no respect for law enforcement? Why is there no respect for the elder voice? Why is there no respect for other human beings?

We all need to be people who show that:

- their word is their bond
- they cannot be bought
- they put character above wealth
- they possess opinions and will
- they are larger than their profession
- they do not hesitate to take chances
- they will not lose their individuality in a crowd
- they will be as honest in the small things as in the big and great things
- they will make no compromise with wrong
- their ambitions are not confined to their own selfish desires

- they will not say they will do something just because everyone else does it
- they are true to their friends through good and bad, in adversity and in prosperity
- they do not believe that crafty hurtful deception and hard-headedness are the best qualities for winning success
- they are not ashamed or afraid to stand for the truth, even when it's unpopular
- they can say no with an emphasis, even when the rest of the world says yes

This world is devolving back to the centuries of no law and order, no reason only revenge, no giving only taking, and no fairness only "mine." I am very concerned about this direction. We all must start at home, one day at a time, one child at a time.

It was done before to turn things around; I just hope we catch it before it's too late.

Beautiful things happen when you distance yourself from negativity.

Do You Know the Key to the Rules for Living?

Functioning every day is different for each of us, based on our individual circumstances. We handle things differently because each of us is unique. We each have different likes and dislikes, habits, routines, needs, and appearance. That is why everyone is so interesting and annoying at the same time. (Sit on a park bench or at the airport or anywhere, and just watch people; you'll see what I mean.)

If we each function differently, then we each must have different rules for living. Having your individual rules for living may come accidentally, through shared information, or from the way we were raised—or maybe we're just winging it. Having rules for living can help us organize, be more efficient at work or at home, get along in a relationship, or get along with other people.

Here are few suggestions for the "Rules for Living" that may help with your standards, morals, or daily functioning:

- If it will brighten someone's day, say it.
- If it's none of your business, don't ask questions.
- If it will tarnish someone's reputation, keep it to yourself.
- If you open it, close it.
- If you turn it on, turn it off.
- If you unlock it, lock it up.
- If you break it, admit it.
- If you can't fix it, call someone who can.
- If you borrow it, return it.
- If you value it, take care of it.
- If you make a mess, clean it up.
- If you move it, put it back.
- If it belongs to someone else and you want to use it, get permission.
- If you don't know how to operate it, leave it alone.

These might seem like basic rules that we all follow, but everyone doesn't have the same Rules for Living. As I was growing up, my father "owned" these rules. He lived by them and made sure the family followed his rules without question. My dad called them "rules of efficiency and common sense." My dad was a listener and was very gentle and kind. He was quiet and a fixer of anything, but he was also a very smart man. Don't make so much work for yourself or others; use common sense and use the Rules for Living.

Your life is a reflection of how you live your life.

Six Phrases to Express a Positive Mind

What is most important in getting along with others? I can narrow it down to the six best phrases to say when you're with other people. Here's the countdown:

6. "I admit I made a mistake."
5. "You did a good job."
4. "What is your opinion?"
3. "Will you please?"
2. "Thank you."
1. "We."

The least important word is "I."

Think before you speak and choose your words carefully. Everything is not about you.

You cannot have a positive life and a negative mind.

How to Determine If You Are a
Good and Kind Person

If your pet could talk, would he or she say you were a good and kind person? We all have our own perceptions of the type of person we are. But are you sure other people see and hear what you do? You may feel you're kind, jolly, and supportive, but that may not be how others perceive you. What you think you are doing may not be what others see and feel. If you think you are being kind, for example, are you presenting yourself that way? Maybe, but maybe not. You may think you look or sound shiny and beautiful, but you may come across as a rusty, tarnished example of your real self.

Here are some guidelines for determining if you are a person with real kindness. You will:

- seek out the good in people
- be the first to say hello
- treat everyone you meet as you want to be treated
- pass on a kindness when you receive a kindness
- make it a habit to do nice things for people who'll never find out
- look for opportunities to make people feel important
- be open and accessible (the next person you meet could become your best friend)
- never underestimate the power of a kind word or deed
- never allow a friend to grieve alone
- be there when people need you
- practice empathy (try to see things from other people's points of view)
- be kinder than necessary

How do you come across? Are you a rusty, tarnished version of yourself or a beautiful shining example of kindness?

Remember, there is also your body language. Not only must you say kind words and act kindly, but your body language must also portray kindness. If you're unsure how other people perceive you, ask someone you trust to be completely honest with you.

Remember that presentation is not always the perception. (Only your dog knows for sure.)

> How you do one thing, is how you do everything. Be aware.

CHAPTER 7

Success

Many of us want to be successful but do not have any idea of how to achieve it. There are so many aspects of success that have nothing to do with having a lot of money, flashy cars, or big houses. Success is all around us every day, yet we may overlook it because we are focused on the wrong image of success. The chapter will give you many examples of what success looks like and where it comes from.

Why Do You Procrastinate?

Do you put things off, wait to do something, or don't feel like doing something now because you don't want to deal with it? Most people will say, "Oh, I just didn't have time," or give a similar excuse, but procrastination is a sign of other issues. Studies have shown procrastination indicates a personal issue, not a lack of time. The following are some of those issues:

- We feel overwhelmed.
- We fear failure.
- We fear success.
- We overestimate the time needed do something.
- We would rather be doing something else.
- We think if we wait long enough, the task will go away.
- We enjoy the last-minute adrenaline rush.

Many of us tell ourselves we don't procrastinate, but some people would rather have a root canal than do whatever they don't want to do. Tackling what you must do, however, without putting it off will really clear your mind. As they say, "Just do it," and get it out of the way.

Unfortunately, the longer you put off something, the harder it is to actually do it. Keeping yourself up-to-date and getting things done on time seems to be the exception for most folks. Take that big weight off your shoulders, and stop letting procrastination control you. The three bad habits that will derail your life and your career are procrastination, excuses, and blame.

If you really want to do something, you'll find a way.
If you don't, you'll find an excuse.

How Did You Feel the Last Time You Said Yes?

How many times have you volunteered for something, saying, "Yes," or "I'll do it," or "I'll make that for you," or "What can I do?" or "Sure, I'd be happy to help"? But after you said yes to someone, did you regret it? Did you gamble away your time? Are you burning the candle at both ends, all because you didn't think about it first?

Saying yes to helping someone is such a selfless, noble offer, and many of us say yes without thinking twice because, of course, we want to help. But if you have said yes to someone, only to find that you never had the time or inclination in the first place, it's quite uncomfortable, isn't it?

What are you suppose to do when you're trying to do the right thing and help others? When you are asked or if you volunteer to do something, to commit yourself, you first need to ask yourself a few questions:

- Do I really understand this commitment?
- Do I have the time, energy, and resources?
- How does this fit with my current goals and priorities right now?
- What impact will this have on me in three to six months, a year, five years, or ten years?
- How will this time spent impact those close to me?
- Who will this help of those I love?
- Could someone else do this better?
- Do I really want to say yes?
- Do I honestly have the energy, drive, and passion to complete this?

Don't put all your eggs in one basket without thinking about it first. Can you see how important it is to stop and ask yourself these questions? If you blurt out *yes* before having time to ask yourself these questions, you will not only be unfair to yourself but to the people who have asked you to do the task you have agreed to do.

Think before you speak. Think once for yourself, think twice for your family, and think a third time for those receiving your commitment. Don't gamble away your time and energy; give it careful thought.

I am learning how to say no and walk away from people and situations that threaten my peace of mind, self-respect, or self-worth.

Are You Doing Too Much?

Whether you are working full time or part time, volunteering, or not working at all, you need to ask yourself this question: "Am I doing too much?"

Look over the questions below and honestly ask yourself where you fit. Do any of these apply to you? You're the only one who can ask and answer the questions, so take a look to see if your lifestyle needs some adjusting or simplifying.

- Do you feel that reading or relaxing is just a waste of time?
- Does your family have trouble finding time to spend with you?
- Have you ever missed an important event in your child's or spouse's life because of a conflicting obligation for which you volunteered?
- Are the storage spaces in your home overflowing because you don't have time to clean out what's been outgrown, broken, or used up?
- Do you spend most of your day feeling tired?
- Are you afraid to say no to an opportunity, fearing it will never come again?
- Do you give your children material items to make up for denying them your time and energy?
- Do you often find you've overscheduled yourself, underestimating the time needed for each event?
- Do you spend the entire day on your devices, only to find the day has gone by while you were on your computer, phone, or other device, scanning through and answering notes?

If you can identify with any of these, maybe you need to start scheduling your time better before you find your entire life is gone.

Sometimes, it's okay if the only thing you do today,
is breathe

214

Who's Really in Control of Your Time?

Wednesdays are a good day to figure out how your time is going this week. Are you getting done what you planned so far this week? No, I am not going to pull out the podium and lecture on time management. I've found that time management is part of your mind-set—when you are driven and passionate about what you are doing because you love it, as I love what I do.

Why not take control of your time? Why would you ever let time take control of you? After all, it's your time. Here are a few suggestions for taking control:

- Reverse schedule

If you live by a schedule, schedule in reverse. Put the real priorities on the calendar first, such as family night or date night. Then everything else can be added. What's most important?

- Honesty

Have you ever found yourself saying yes to a project in the hopes that a weekend will suddenly and magically hold in reserve the ten extra hours you would need to complete that project? Newsflash: you can't manufacture time. Be honest about your limitations before you wear yourself out. It *is* okay to say no; no one will freak out.

- Be in charge

Being in charge can be scary, but you have to be in control of yourself. Learn to think through each time commitment completely—that means the whole start-to-finish time period. Give yourself time to think by saying, "Can I let you know tomorrow?" Remember who is in charge of your time. Is it you or the person who's asking for a time commitment?

- Drop it

If you spend two fewer days each month helping at your child's school as a lunch monitor, room parent, or carpool participant, those two days will free you up for a lunch date with your spouse or friend. You may let someone down, but, again, who is in charge of your time? You cannot be everywhere, so drop even one thing from your schedule.

- Make a list

Think about your commitments and make a list of them. Start with a week at a time and then a month at a time until you learn and get used to your new posture. You need a little time to get used to who is really in charge of your time. When you make your commitment list, make it large enough so you can't miss it. Then place your list next to wherever you usually make your commitments—next to the phone, on your computer monitor, next to your laptop, or on the calendar. This is a visual reminder of your involvement and will make you think twice before you add something else.

- Opinion

Sometimes you are so involved with you own world of duties it's hard to take a step back to see how you're doing. Ask for an honest perspective from your spouse or close friends about your limitations. Ask them to comment on how you're using your time and what they see that may be robbing you of your time. If you ask for an honest opinion, however, you have to be ready to accept their honest answer. (It's not like asking them if you butt looks fat in those pants.)

- Decisions

Be honest with yourself and decide what is truly urgent. Rather than think, *I must get this done now*, try putting it off. Walk away and think about it before doing it. Most "urgent" needs really aren't that urgent (excluding life-or-death emergencies).

- Relax

Have you ever heard this: "Be, rather than do." Try this for an evening. Think. Pray. Relax in a chair (even doze if you want). Let me ask you again: who is really in charge of your time?

Time has a wonderful way of showing us what really matters

Why Do I Never Get Anything Done?

Where are your thoughts right now? My thoughts have been all over the place. Have you ever had those days when you started one project, and before you know it, you look up and find you have started multiple projects that are scattered all about? I have done this; I sat there a moment, looking around, and actually said out loud, "This is not like me at all. What just happened here?"

I am naturally quite focused and specific about my projects, but one morning my desk looked like it had exploded with thoughts and ideas. For me, that was clearly a teachable moment. If you listen carefully, you will be able to hear which of those thoughts and ideas speaks to you the loudest. If you don't hear anything, try again because you are clearly not sitting quietly enough or long enough with an open mind.

Are your ideas in one place, or are they scattered? When you find yourself going from one task to another and another, you think you've done a lot today—until you stop and look around you. You started the day straightening up the kitchen, then suddenly stopped and found yourself in the living room, and then you're in the garage. You see all these different rabbit trails where you started one thing and wound up in another area. None of what you started in each area was finished before you moved on to something else.

It might be in your office, where you begin to write an idea down but then start making notes about something that popped in your head. Now you're in the file cabinet because you were looking for something and decided to clean it out. Then the phone rings, and you suddenly commit by saying, "I'll do it right now." Work is always a famous place for rabbit trails—little starts and stops and turns to something else.

You are working so hard, moving everywhere, covering a lot of ground—but you haven't accomplished one thing. Does this sound familiar? How can you stop these rabbit trails to nowhere? We all have different methods of completing a to-do list for the day, but we get distracted by anything that pops up in our minds at any given moment.

What you *want* to get done on any given day will not be what you actually get done for that day. Unless you are in the military—and I have been in the military as an officer, so I can speak to this—you will not have an exact list of orders and an itinerary with the expectations you will complete. You will not complete the list of tasks you thought you would—no surprise there.

To prevent the rabbit trail dilemmas, you have to be focused and alert each moment on what you are doing.

1. Don't set up your to-do list for the day the night before. Tomorrow is eight to twelve hours away, and a lot of things will change from the time you make that list until you actually get started. Give yourself some time to get your thoughts together in the morning, and keep your list short.

2. Be realistic with your list. If you have ad copy to write, a report to finish, and a presentation to prepare and already have six prospect calls to make before noon, you'll be lucky to even finish one of those tasks. Writing ad copy takes creative time to come up with an idea, display images, and keep the content within the spot. To finish a report that's already started, you have to mentally bring your thoughts back into what you were actually thinking when you were writing the report idea. Presentation preparation requires time for gathering ideas, even if you cut down the number of key points from six to three. Making six prospect calls is not something you want to rush—these can be time-consuming.

3. If your day will be at home, you also need to be realistic with your list. If you have the house to clean, shopping to get done, prescriptions to pick up, and paint colors to pick out, what in the world are you thinking? That list has time-consuming activities, each of which has the ability to require more time than you think. How many times have you combined cleaning the house and grocery shopping without running out of time by the end of the day? These always take a lot longer than you allow for. After all that running around, will you have a clear mind and thought process to allow you to pick out paint colors? Where are you going wrong here?

There really is no right or wrong way to get yourself organized. You already know what you need to do—*slow down* and be still. The problem is we all need slow down, step back, and chill out. We are all busy, we are all on a deadline of some sort, and we all have to get it done "yesterday." Do you really have to run at full throttle all the time?

Why are we always at a dead run? Why are we packing in as many things as we can into one day? You already know it's not going to all get done, so why do you continue to try to do it? Why are you in such a hurry to get that list completed, or get that report done, or quickly get those calls made? Where are you going in such a rush? Is it to the next thing on your list or the next pile on your desk?

You know what you need to do. You are in such a hurry, with your head down, looking at your lists, looking at your paperwork, checking your watch, your speedometer, your cell phone, your computer. Haven't you forgotten something?

I read something a long time ago that has stuck with me: "Don't say you don't have enough time. You have exactly the same number of hours per day that were available for Helen Keller, Louis Pasteur, Michelangelo, Mother Teresa, Leonardo da Vinci, Thomas Jefferson, and Albert Einstein." And none of those individuals had cell phones, computers, cars, printers, copiers, or even indoor plumbing!

We all need to breathe, to slow down, to just be still, to look up and take the time to look around us.

We are given only one shot at this. We have only one life, and folks, this is it, and it's right now. We are, at this very moment in the middle of the life we were given. Ask yourself if you're living the life you want. Is running yourself to death to get your list done or your paperwork caught up what you really want out of this life you have" On the way to work, school, the store, day care, or office this morning, did you look around an notice the environment, the world of wonder that we live in? At the speed with which many of us go through every day, we will someday look back and realize we spent or entire lives trying to keep up and meet deadlines for someone else's life.

Whatever you are doing, whatever your responsibilities, or however you live your life every day, take the time to stop and just listen carefully to yourself. Give yourself the time to hear your thoughts. Stop and listen to your thoughts, listen to your heart, enjoy what's around you, and live your life. You *can* complete a reasonable to-do list and enjoy what's around you.

Give yourself balance so you don't wind up missing out on all the things that happen to you while you were busy doing something else. If you slow down and consistently put your life as your first priority, people may say that you've changed. Of course you will have changed; it may simply be because you stopped living your life their way.

> *"Twenty years from now you will be more disappointed by the things that you didn't do than by the ones you did do."*
>
> —Mark Twain

How to Find the Real Meaning of Success

Many people think they know what it takes to be successful—money. The more capital, the bigger and better your success.

Money does help, but to be really successful you have to know the true keys to success. If you don't have them, you are done before you even get started. Below you'll find those keys to success. If you follow these consistently, believe in them, and practice them, money won't matter.

How to Find the Real Meaning of Success

- Find the best in others.
- Appreciate beauty.
- Give of oneself.
- Win the respect of intelligent people and the affection of children.
- Laugh often and love much.
- Earn the approval of honest critics and endure the betrayal of false friends.
- Play and laugh with enthusiasm and sing with praise.
- Leave the world a better place, whether by a healthy child, a garden patch, or a redeemed social condition.
- Know that even one life has breathed easier because you lived.

This is to have succeeded. Success truly is not about the money; it's about what is inside you. Success is about your authentic self, how you have helped others, and how you have given of yourself to make someone else's life better. Success is about the transformation of you that shines upon another person to make his or her life worth living.

Success isn't about how much money you make. It's about the difference you make in people's lives.

Three Simple Secrets to Success

Everyone seems to have his or her recipe for success, "Just follow these twelve steps …" But what if you don't have time to take a class, travel to a seminar, or buy a program to learn those steps? If you want to succeed, you must find the path to your desires, and sometimes you'll have to stretch and compromise for it.

I'm going to make it extremely simple for you. Here are three simple secrets to success:

- Be willing to learn new things.
- Be able to take in new information quickly.
- Be able to get along with and work with other people in a positive manner.

That's it. That is the foundation of succeeding. No tricks, no hoops, no gimmicks.

If you do not have a good foundation of being willing, being open, and being positive, you will never succeed in anything. Period.

Don't think of cost. Think of value.

What Type of Personality Does an Entrepreneur Have?

There seems to be a huge misconception that you have to be highly educated and wealthy to be an entrepreneur. This is totally false. I'm going to share what my friend and mentor, Erica Udeanu, taught me about being an entrepreneur.

An entrepreneur is someone who organizes a business and takes the risk of running his or her own business. Anyone can be an entrepreneur, but the decision to become an entrepreneur is something only you can answer for yourself. I'm going to share the traits I have learned of an entrepreneur; see if you have these qualities. The list is long, but you'll need every one these qualities if you want to be a successful entrepreneur:

- courage—tenacity and persistence
- drive—a high degree of self-motivation
- goals—a sense of direction
- knowledge—a thirst for it
- good health—taking care of your body
- honesty—especially intellectual
- optimism—positive attitude
- judgment—knowing the wise from the foolish
- enthusiasm—excitement about life
- taking chances—willingness to risk failure
- dynamism—energy
- enterprise—willingness to tackle tough jobs
- persuasion—ability to sell
- outgoingness—friendly
- patient, yet impatient—patient with others, yet impatient with the status quo
- adaptability—capable of change
- perfectionism—desire to achieve excellence
- humor—ability to laugh at yourself and others.
- versatility—broad interests and skills

- curiosity—interested in people and things
- self-identity—self-esteem and self-sufficiency
- realism/idealism—occupied by reality but guided by ideals
- imagination—seeking new ideas, combinations, and relationships
- communication—being articulate
- receptive—alert

Do you have what it takes to be an entrepreneur? Do you want to work for your own dreams instead of someone else's dreams? Of course you do. All these qualities are right inside of you.

Here are a few more thoughts about being an entrepreneur:

You can work full time or part-time from home without the expensive overhead of property and taxes, without commuting and deteriorating your car, and without having to find expensive day care for your children. Best of all, there's no daily stress of a boss or coworkers.

How do you learn what to do? Are there risks? It's easy to learn, and whose life are you living—yours or your employer's? Is it financially stable? There's no guarantee, but ask yourself if your job and financial status with your employer is stable.

Happiness is not determined by what's happening around you but by what's happening inside you. Most people depend on others to gain happiness, but it always comes from within.

Did you know it's easier to succeed than to fail? Isn't it easier to learn and master something than to keep failing and losing nothing and not having to do all that work? I'll tell you why I believe it's so much easier to succeed than to fail.

Failing at something has more to do with limitations you've put on yourself. You've come up short and didn't get it, likely because you gave up. When you were a child, did your parents or teachers ever say, "There is nothing you cannot do"? Regardless of your age or abilities, there is *nothing* you cannot do—if you put your mind to it.

If you make a partial attempt at something, you'll never do it, you won't finish, and you'll fail. You'll fail because you put your physical body into the motions, but you just went through the steps. When you do something with determination in your mind that you *will* get this,

225

you *are* going to learn this, and you *are* going to learn or do something new, you will because you've already programmed yourself that you're going to do this.

What if something is too hard, heavy, complicated, or not for you? *That* is a decision you've made and put in your mind—that you can't do it and that you'll fail at the task that you're going to try. It's not your physical ability; it's your mind and emotional ability. Don't say, "I'll try"; just do it!

Look at these reasons why it's easier to succeed:

- It's easier to succeed because the money spent to fail must be spent again to succeed.
- It's easier to succeed because failure costs a high price of time when you have to do a job or task over again.
- It's easier to succeed because success eliminates the agony and frustration of defeat.
- It's easier to succeed because a person's credibility decreases with each failure, making it harder to succeed the second time.
- It's easier to succeed because joy and expressions of affirmation come from succeeding, whereas feelings of discouragement and discontent accompany failure.

Can you see the pattern here? It's not about the money you invest to learn something in order to succeed or your physical abilities. It's about the time and emotions it costs you by not making your mind up in the first place that you *can* succeed.

One last thought to consider: you've probably seen heroic stories on TV or in the paper about someone being trapped under a car, and someone came along and lifted that car off that person. Most of us can't just walk up to a car and lift it up. But when an emergency happens—someone is trapped under a car, seconds from dying—an individual rushes to help without giving it a second thought and is able to lift the car. While this person may struggle to carry groceries in the house, he or she acts on unconscious activity and just does the act by trying. The individual has already put his or her mind into a "can and will do it" mode, not an "I'll try" mode. Amazingly, the person lifts the car without hurting himself or herself.

Your strength, abilities, successes, and failures all come from you mind, not from your physical abilities. Your mind is governed by what you have decided to do, what you have fed it, and what you have programmed it to do at any given moment.

Whether you feel at the bottom of your life with all the things that are going wrong, or you feel at the top of your game in business, success should have the same meaning. It might be hard to see this when nothing is going right for you, but realize that most people have grown up in this world with the belief that success means being rich, the head of a company, a degreed professional, living in a mansion, driving snazzy cars, and fulfilling their dreams.

But that is not what success is.

Success is defined as "the achievement of something attempted" and "gaining fame and prosperity," and "succeeding fully or in accordance to one's desires." Success is an accomplishment, achievement, triumph, or a victory of what we set out to do. But there's more to success than tangible achievements. Success is actually within you. It's what you feel within your heart and soul. Success is what your image portrays naturally and simply because of your beliefs.

Today I am successful. Tomorrow I will be successful.
Every day I am successful.

How to Know the Difference
between Failing and Failure

When everything falls apart and our world as we knew it starts crumbling down around us, we know we've failed. We look at all we did and all we had and realize we're just a failure.

The dictionary definition of *fail* is "to be unsuccessful, to cease in function." It defines *failure* as "the act of failing, someone who has failed." We can't dispute that, but I want you to know that those are not the real definitions.

To fail is *not* the same as being a failure. Consider this:

- You may have many failings, yet still be far from being a failure.
- To fail is not the disgrace everyone thinks it is. To make an error is to do nothing more than to join the human race.
- Failure is only a temporary setback:
- Failure is never the final chapter of the book of your life unless you give up and quit.
- Nothing worthwhile is ever achieved without running the risk of failure:
- Anyone who risks everything to try to achieve something truly worthwhile and fails is anything but a disgraceful failure.
- Failure is a natural preparation for success.

Strange though it may seem, success is much more difficult to live with than is failure. Every failing brings with it the possibility of something greater. Analyze failure under whatever circumstances you choose, and you will discover some seeds for turning failure into success. What you do with failures in your life is up to you.

- Failure is either a blessing or a curse, depending on the individual's reaction or response to it.
- Failings are opportunities to learn how to do things better the next time, to learn where the pitfalls are and how to avoid them.

- The best possible thing to do with failure is to learn all you can from it.
- If you "fail" at something, immediately turn that into a teachable moment for yourself.
- You don't learn unless you make some failures along the way.
- Never let those mishaps cause you to give up; learn all you can from it and move on.
- Sometimes good things fall apart so better things can fall together.

Just be patient. Sometimes you have to go through the worst, to get to the best

CHAPTER 8

Life

Life is tough and does not come with instructions, so we have to figure things out as we go. The truth is, life is what we make it. Good or bad, we can have more control of the results than we think. We have no control of what happens every day, but we do have control of how we react to it and deal with the situations that cross our paths. This chapter will give you a view of what can happen and how we should carefully choose how to deal with life's many possibilities.

"Why Can't I Just Do It Over Again!"

Have you ever heard anyone say, "Why can't I just do it over again?" Maybe you've said it yourself. But such opportunities rarely happen. We learn from our mistakes, so getting a "do-over" would be an awesome privilege, wouldn't it?

I once did a study regarding that very thought. I interviewed random people, random patients, random family members, all of various age groups, over the course of a year. There was nothing scientific about it; instead, I just asked them to complete a simple phrase. All were asked privately and at different times.

Interestingly, the answers from hundreds of people were quite similar. Even more interesting was that their responses were also much like those from a survey done more recently than mine that used a similar type of phrase.

My study asked the participants to complete the following: "If I had it to do over again …" Here are the results of my study on "do-overs." These are the real answers from participants.

If I had it to do over again …

- I would listen more, even to the youngest child.
- I would pay more attention to little things, deeds, and words of love and kindness.
- I would do more with my children.
- I would be more encouraging and give more praise.
- I would show love to my wife [husband] more in front of my children.
- I would be more honest about my own weaknesses and stop pretending perfection.
- I would laugh with my children and friends more at our mistakes and our joys.
- I would pray differently for my family.
- I would enjoy life more and work less.
- I would be in less of a hurry all the time.
- I would spend more time to *be* in the moment.
- I would believe more in myself.
- I would thank God more for providing for me.
- I would make time for others.

What did this tell me? This simple study told me that we all know the right things to do or say, but we don't take the time to just do it. Instead, these are the afterthoughts we have, although we really do know better.

Imagine someone like me randomly coming up to you and asking you how you would finish a simple phrase. Let me try this one more time. In one short sentence, what would you say to finish the phrase, "If I had it to do over again …"?

It is never too late to be what you might have been.

Why Didn't Anybody Tell Me This Before?

As we grow up, we are told many things and we learn a lot. We are sponge-like as we absorb information. It's interesting, though. how easily so many people never seem to hear the part about life within us. We can understand a well-put explanation about how to operate a basic computer, drive a car, or follow a recipe (well, some of us). Many of us are very skilled with more complicated technical things like motors, machines, computer hardware, instruments, music, or dance. Those sorts of things are for those who are driven to learn them; they "get it."

So, what happened to listening and understanding how we handle life from within ourselves? Here's what we didn't "hear" when we were told about the basics of life.

We do not understand the following:

- peace, until faced with conflict
- trust, until we are betrayed
- love, until it is lost
- hope, until confronted with doubts
- faith, until it is tested
- joy, until we face sorrow

These are basic personal development thoughts, but it should not take a devastating incident to learn these or how to use them, often for the first time. These are daily staples everyone should make a point of having within himself or herself. These are the "go-to" thoughts and beliefs that hold us up and together. They require daily practice, understanding, and exercise. Be sure you carry these understandings and use them properly, as you need them, every day.

Channel your personal energy to things you can influence and control.

How to Know What Contented Living Is

Sometimes being down can distort your view on the simplest things. When faced with so many negative issues, we have times when we don't know which end is up.

Everyone you talk to will have a different version of what *contented living* means, and that is perfectly fine because we are all different. I am referring to contented living only as living while being satisfied within yourself. That doesn't mean living to please others or to live a certain way because you have to. I'm talking about living every day in a way that gives you that inner peace. This contentment should come from inside you; it's a contentment that you believe in.

Some people refer this as mind-set living, which is really a very good name for contented living because your mind-set comes from within your beliefs. Be sure if you're living a mind-set life style that your thoughts and beliefs are positive and action-oriented.

What follows are ideas I had to master for my own contented living, when I was pulling myself up from my life-changing issues. They worked to bring me back to the success I have today. How do you know what contented living is? You'll know you have it when you have the following:

- strength enough to battle difficulties and overcome them
- health enough to make work a pleasure
- wealth enough to support your needs
- grace enough to confess your sins and forgive yourself
- patience enough to untangle things in your life until some good is accomplished
- clarity enough to see some good in your neighbor
- love enough to move you to be useful and helpful to others
- faith enough to make real the life that you have been given
- hope enough to remove all anxious fears confronting your future

Remember that just because you may have had hard times or have been given a diagnosis, that is no reason to surrender and give up!

These are things you need to believe in yourself. Give yourself a break and just work on *you* while you are trying to get real with yourself. You are building these things—strength, health, wealth, grace, and so on—within yourself. It's part of reorganizing your thinking about yourself.

I know you've heard this before, but you have to love yourself before anyone else can love or respect you. The list above are some of the essentials to help you do that.

> *Happiness is not determined by what's happening around you but rather what's happening inside you. Most people depend on others to gain happiness, but it always comes from within.*

Do You Know What It Takes to Have a Better Life?

We all want to have a wonderful life, don't we? But is there some sort of secret to it? It's not really a "secret" at all, and it's not about luck, four-leaf clovers, or having a rabbit's foot. Living a better life is really easy for anyone to accomplish. It requires only that you change your thinking, your mind-set, and your actions. This occurs when you do the following:

- Feel positive emotions.
- Think positive thoughts.
- Focus on the positive in people.
- Offer positive prayers.
- Speak positive words.
- Practice positive actions.

If you feel and think negatively, focus only on negative people, talking negatively to others, and act negatively, you will have a negative life. You have complete control of how you act, talk, think, feel, and carry yourself. If you want to feel good about yourself, then act, talk, think, feel, and carry yourself in a positive way. You'll have more energy, less stress, and more happiness, and you'll sleep better when you're positive.

Be positive to live a better life. You won't regret it.

Living life to the fullest and meeting your goals and dreams and having what you want all boils down to the simplest of thoughts. You can pay a lot of money to attend a conference to learn the "Secrets of Success" or "The Answer to Your Life's Questions." You can shadow the leaders of the world to pick their brains for their formula for the happiest way to live. Or you can subscribe to the most famous individual's concept of happiness.

But your own circumstance will be unchanged because you've had the secrets within you the whole time. For your own success, business, money, dreams and happiness, it all boil down to a better life by learning new things, understanding new information and getting along with others.

You are the key; you just need to be you. There are no magic potions, formulas, or tricks of the trade. You can do it yourself but just do whatever it takes to get yourself where you want to go.

Believe in yourself, and everyone will believe in you.

How to Find the Key to a Better Life

That's such a bold statement, isn't it? It sounds like a pot of gold found on your journey through life will suddenly make you a better you. Why do we make things so hard and try to find the quick fix and remedy? Have you wondered what the remedy really is?

The answer is *you*. Yes, you have the answer that unlocks the door to your better life. To see how to find the key to a better life, just look in the mirror. You have the key inside of you. Are you ready to put it to proper use?

Here is how to find the key to a better life:

We each have a mental image of ourselves—what we look like, how smart we are, what are feelings are, how we behave, what our abilities are, how we react to various things, what our outlook on things is, and what our personalities are. Remember, this is your own interpretation of how you are to others every day.

If you believe that you're intimidated by others, feel inferior to everyone, and are not as good, talented, or smart as others, that is how they will perceive you. If you think you're not as attractive as others, you don't dress as stylishly, and your hair looks terrible all the time, then that is how you'll come across to everyone.

If you believe, however, that you're an outgoing, perky, positive go-getter who loves to help people, that you have a lot to offer, and you look good, that's how you'll come across to everyone.

Your own self-image in your mind has to have your actions, feelings, behavior, abilities, and beliefs. Others will see you based on your posture and your frame of mind and attitude. If your self-image is of negative beliefs about yourself, then you'll project and carry yourself in a negative way. If your self-image is of positive beliefs about yourself, you will project and carry yourself in a positive manner. Simply put, when you act like the kind of person you believe yourself to be, that is how you'll be seen. If you act like a success, you will be a success. If you act like a failure, you will find some way to fail, despite all your good intentions.

The key to a better life is in knowing that it's all within you. Go look in the mirror and ask yourself how you want to have a better life. The answer is already inside of you; you just have to believe.

Your energy introduces you before you even speak

How Well Do You Understand Life?

Life doesn't always happen the way you plan. You get up and take a step back or two, which causes you to be late, or you're handed more work than you expected. Sometimes life takes an unexpected turn that throws you off guard. But that's not what I getting at here.

Sometimes it takes a life-changing setback before you can truly understand the meaning of life. Until that life-changing devastation happens to you, you really don't understand how much you take for granted. Until you experience such devastation, whether physical, emotional, or both, you'll never understand the value of life.

How well do you understand life? I believe you won't understand many things until you actually go through them. For example, you won't understand:

- joy, until you face sorrow
- faith, until it is tested
- peace, until you are faced with conflict
- trust, until you are betrayed
- love, until it's lost
- hope, until you are confronted with doubts
- courage, until you have to get back on your feet
- belief, until you've had to depend on yourself
- perseverance, until it was all up to you
- life, until yours has changed forever

Remember, if you are facing devastation, loss, depression, or challenges, and now you feel like you can't get back up, you can and will.

I understand because I have been there. I too have hit bottom from a devastating accident. I too have had to start over physically, emotionally, and financially. Was it easy for me? Of course not. It was the hardest thing I've ever done in my life. Why am I telling you this?

I want you to understand four things:

- Do not take your life for granted.
- Do not assume tomorrow will be here.

- Do not think you are alone.
- Do not ever give up.

Adversities in life will make you stronger, smarter, and full of character if you handle your climb back up with gratitude and humility. Don't wait until something happens to you to understand and be grateful for your life. Take each moment and each day to understand the true meaning of life, and never take tomorrow for granted.

Challenges are what make life interesting; overcoming them is what makes life meaningful.

What Are You Doing for Yourself Today?

Regardless of what you're going through—loss, life-changing events, overwhelming issues, stress from work or lack of money—you can still do things every day for yourself. You must take the time you need to find things that will offset these overwhelming issues that are weighing on you, even if it's for a short time, but at least you will have taken the moments to do something for yourself.

Whether you are a top millionaire, are homeless, are grieving, are successful in your own business, or are struggling to make ends meet, the most important thing is that you take care of you. Doing something for yourself brings an internal smile to your body, mind, and soul. Doing little positive things for yourself not only gives you internal peace, but those around you will benefit from your taking care of yourself.

Here are a few simple things that will make your heart smile:

- Applaud others' successes.
- Help others exercise daily.
- Keep a positive attitude.
- Read a variety of things for thirty minutes a day that will give you strength and hope.
- Play with the children.
- Enjoy nature again.
- Laugh heartily and out loud.
- Play with your pet.
- Plant a little garden.
- Take a class.
- Count your blessings every day.
- Take a risk.
- Say hello to someone you don't know.
- Open a door for someone.
- Get a pet.
- Eat healthily.
- Give your time generously to others.

There is nothing but joy in these activities, but if you're saying "I don't have time," then you especially need to make the time for some of these. Being on a dead run is harming you physically. If you don't pay attention to yourself first, you won't be worth anything to anyone else. If you are so down in the dumps that these ideas don't even appeal to you, I want to let you know that I was further down than you are now, and I had to find something to give to myself to change my outlook from within.

In order to start pulling yourself back up, you have to start from deep within yourself to change your negative thinking. If you don't change your internal negatives, you'll never be able to pull yourself out of what you're going through. Trust me; I have been exactly where you are now.

The only way I was able to get to where I am now—to be successful in what I'm doing—was to start deep within myself by starting to feed and fertilize myself with internal smiles and joy for myself. By doing these positive things every day, faithfully, regardless of how I felt, those little seeds of internal positive joys started to grow and became my everyday habits.

What you sow is what you will reap. What you plant and feed within yourself is what will grow, and that is exactly what you'll become.

"Whatever you hold inside your mind on a consistent
basis, is exactly what you will experience in your life."
—Tony Robbins

How Well Do You Know Yourself?

To function well in life, you must know yourself, to succeed, to grow, to love, to flourish, to thrive. My question to you is, how well do you really know yourself? If you don't know yourself, what you're made of, how you think, and your likes and dislikes, how will you ever know what your dreams, passions, and visions are? Simply put, you won't.

Those around you know how you project yourself, even your pets. To really know yourself, have you ever asked yourself these questions?

- What do you want most?
- What do you think about the most?
- How do you spend your money?
- What do you do with your leisure time?
- Who is the company you enjoy being with?
- Whom and what do you admire, and why?
- What do you laugh at, or who makes you laugh?

These should be the basics of your likes, thoughts, desires, enjoyment, and personal finances. If you don't know these answers, you need to dig deeper to find out. In order to love yourself, which is what you have to do before you can ever love anyone else, you first need to know about yourself. Only then will the rest follow for your second step—believing in yourself. Once you believe in yourself, you can do anything.

You will never become who you want to be if you keep blaming everyone else for who you are now.

Wisdom for Success from Life's Lessons

Previously, I made the statement that the educational achievements we collect through college degrees and diplomas, are not wisdom—at least, not the sort of wisdom I am referring to.

As we grow, we learn wisdom through life's lessons. We learn that bringing home a dandelion freshly picked out of the yard for our mom made her smile. That worked out so well that the next time we picked a bunch of dandelions and presented our bouquet. That scored hugs and kisses from Mom.

We learn that regardless of our relationship with our parents, we miss them after they die.

We learn, through trial and error, that if we want to do something positive for our children, we should just improve our marriages.

We learn that life sometimes gives us a second chance.

We learn that if we pursue happiness, we won't seem to find it. But if we focus on our family, the needs of others, our work, meeting new people, and doing the best we can every day, happiness will find us.

We learn that whenever we decide something with true kindness from our hearts, we usually make the right decision.

We learn, when become older, that even if we have pain, we don't have to be one.

For me, I've learned that every day I should reach out and touch someone. People love human touch—holding hands with my other half, a warm hug for my friends, or even a friendly soft pat on the back. I've also learned just sharing a smile with people I don't even know can change their whole day—and mine too.

But mostly, I've learned that I still have a lot to learn.

The wisdom we learn from our daily lessons is the most valuable education we will ever obtain.

Grasp your life's lessons and hold them close to your heart. You'll never know when you will need them within your life and to project yourself in more success.

Everything that has ever happened in your life is preparing you for a moment that has yet to come.

The Wisdom of Life's Lessons

The little things in my life that I have gone through and experienced are my "degrees." Let me reword that another way: all my post-high school accomplishments—college degrees, graduate diplomas, licenses, certifications, and national, local, and military honors and awards of achievements are not what has given me the wisdom I have today.

Paper accomplishments are necessary tickets to navigate through your business life, but these educational achievements are not what it takes to learn about life. Ask yourself this: did my undergrad or graduate degree make me the person I am today? No, it did not. You cannot be taught wisdom.

In fact according to the American Heritage Dictionary; "Wisdom is understanding, common sense, good judgement and learned knowledge".

We learn wisdom through the lessons in our lives starting when we were just kids ourselves. Here are some of Life's Lessons we learned:

Don't call others names, don't us bad words, go to church, smile, hold hands when crossing the street, put your dirty dishes in the sink, don't burp in public, don't hit others, share what you have, don't chew with your mouth open, don't pick off scabs, say please and thank you, be nice to old people, brush your teeth, clean your room, close your eyes when you pray, listen …

Maybe some learn other things but for me, this was the basics of life things to know and go by. We all learn things through time, but if the basics are not learned as children, life's lessons as we go through adulthood will be a difficult task for many.

These are life lessons that give us wisdom, and wisdom is the most valuable free lesson of all. Cherish yours.

Nothing in life has any meaning except the meaning we give it.

"How Can I Believe in Anything When Nothing Is Going Right?"

When things start going wrong, why does it feel like an avalanche of problems?

"My car broke down and is in the shop, then I bounced a check at the dentist's office, and my boss has been on my case about being more productive. How can I think straight when my landlord is after me for my past-due rent?"

People are drowning in problems and seem to have no way out. The above situations are all too common, but there are solutions. There is a light at the end of the tunnel. There is already a mechanism in place to change your situation. The answer lies within you. You have the keys to your issues and resolutions. Do you think it takes money to resolve your problems? It very well may be, but it first starts with you.

How you think about an issue, how you handle an issue, and how you face an issue has everything to do with how you resolve it.

I've said it above and even earlier in this book, but I'll repeat it for you here: *you* have the keys to your issues and resolutions. How you believe in yourself, how you value yourself, and how you set your opinions about yourself is exactly how you're going to work through what you have in front of you.

The following points are what you should believe in and value. Read each one and think about it for a moment, even if things are looking rough for you at the time.

How to Change Your Mishaps into Working for You

Your new motto: "What I believe in and value"
Hope: facilitate the growth and success of others.
Love: embrace people with openness and acceptance.
Impact: practice the courage to take risks.
Grace: treasure life as a gift from God.
Strength: fight the good fight, hard.
Human dignity: first understand before passing judgment.

Integrity: acquire enough wisdom to be humble.

Fun: have at least one hearty laugh each day.

Honesty: always speak the truth about yourself and others.

Self-opinion: have an exalted self-opinion that you *will* be fine.

Believe you can make that shot, believe you can turn things around, believe and value your inner strength. If you can develop the belief and values like those listed above, then from inside yourself you can change the way you look at your problems.

"But I need money, not words!"

Think back about the section in this book where I discussed the 'Subconscious Minds, your creative mechanism". You will have the things you need, but if you don't believe in yourself, you never will have the money you need to resolve your issues. If you don't change your opinion about yourself, you will stay as you are and continue to have self-pity and resentment, adding to your misfortune. You'll be rich in negative thoughts about yourself.

Do not add to the negative issues around you. Believe and know you can and will get through these, and let it motivate you to just do it.

Start looking at things differently with the "I can do this" attitude, instead of the "what am I going to do" attitude. You can do and overcome anything if you just *believe.*

Limitations live only in our minds. But if we use our imaginations, our possibilities become limitless.

"How can I possibly believe in anything when nothing's going right?"

Haven't you had days when you've wanted to just scream, when nothing was going the right way? Boy, I have, and I've seen those around me face these times too. Sometimes you just think you'd be better off going back to bed before you hurt yourself or anyone else. You are not alone here. So how in the world can you get this free-fall to turn around? First of all, *stop*!

You know now what can go wrong, so it's out of your system. Start over with a "fresh" thought and mind-set. Just take a mulligan—that's a missed shot in golf, like you just made when things just fell apart. You get to start over with a free swing, without a penalty.

Okay, now regroup and get yourself under control. But first, consider these few thoughts:

Say to yourself, out loud:

- I believe in the sun, even though it's not shining.
- I believe in love, even when it isn't shown.
- I believe in God, even when he doesn't speak.
- I believe in myself, even when I am weakened and I stumble.
- I believe in myself, and I know I can and will do this.

Believing in yourself is all the tools you need to do anything that you have a passion to do. Your belief in yourself will get you everything you want. It's not rocket science, it's not expensive, and it's not hard. Just believe in yourself. No one else knows what's in your heart the way you do.

Believe in yourself, even if no one else believes in you.

Are You Being Destructive?

In reality, no two people have the exact style, personality, drive, or deep common interests. This is why we have "similar" interests. The same can be said for our habits and personalities, but "habits and personalities" are where the problems begin. Many have a certain plan for how to make it, how to get ahead, how to get to the top, whether in life or in business.

There are billions of us in the world, and that is how many ways the roads are being traveled to get to where we want to be. I'm not here to tell you how to get there or how to set up your GPS. Instead, I'll give you some thoughts about a few destructive mistakes that will certainly blow your plans for accomplishment right out of the water. They are as follows:

- attempting to compel others to believe and live as you do
- neglecting development and refinement of the mind and not acquiring the habit of reading and studying personal development
- refusing to set aside trivial preferences
- insisting that a thing is impossible because you cannot accomplish it
- the tendency to worry about things that cannot be changed or corrected
- the delusion that personal gain is made by crushing others

These are only a few of the very destructive mistakes to make on your journey to conquer what you want to achieve in your life. If any of these pertain to you, stop and change that mistake immediately. If you don't know why, then you probably already have taken the wrong turn and you will not find your road to true success.

Solid, long-lasting success and accomplishments are achieved only by the belief you consistently have in yourself and the destructive mistakes you avoid while getting yourself to where you want to be.

Success is the sum of small positive efforts, repeated day in and day out.

Growing Old Gracefully.

Time is not on our side. It's clicking away, second by second, moment by moment. One thing we can all agree on is that we are getting older every day. So, what's the remedy for aging?

There isn't any remedy; there's no anti-aging pill, cream, or surgery (despite what some pay thousands for). These artificial remedies are truthfully only to make you feel better, to make you feel as though you are in control. Sorry, but that's the truth. Embrace your experience; you've earned it. You paid the price through blood, sweat, and tears.

What can we do about getting older? Accept it, live life to the fullest, appreciate others, and love yourself. There are some things, however, that you *can* control. Read them, let them marinate in your mind, and put them to good use in your situations.

I call these "growing old gracefully":

Fear less; hope more.

Eat less; chew more.

Talk less; say more.

Hate less; love more.

Interrupt less; listen more.

Resent less; engage more.

Expect less; enjoy more.

Take less; give more,

Regardless of your age at this moment, these are things live by now. By the time you are elderly, these thoughts for growing old gracefully will just come naturally.

You will never become who you want to be if you keep
blaming everyone else for who you are now.

CHAPTER 9

Hope

There are many facets that effect hope in us, ranging from courage to belief to another person's and our own approach for what we have suddenly been dealt. You have more to do with the success of your belief than you realize, and what gives hope differs among every person. Many times, hearing something a different way but with the same message is all it takes for you to build your own hope. Other times, it's watching others go through their issues that gives you a sudden spark in yourself. Whatever ignites within you, this chapter may be just enough to fill the void you have within yourself.

Thinking Like a Good Friend Will Resolve Things Differently

Everyone makes mistakes, says or does something wrong, and hurts someone without thinking. You've done that, haven't you? You also know how it feels when someone does that to you. At some point in life, someone said something hurtful to you that made you step back and say to yourself, "Wow." If not, you're lucky because when that happens, the hurt that you feel can change an entire relationship if you don't handle it properly.

So what do you do? Wait for an apology?

What if that person did apologize. Would you really forgive him or

252

her? What if the person acted like nothing was wrong, much less didn't apologize?

You may be able to forgive, but that stinger, the hurt or pain and the changed image you have about that person, may not recover.

Now what? How do you handle a situation like this because you really do care about that person? No one can tell you what to do in your situation, but I'll share very basic guidelines that might give you something to work on and treating these situations as a 'Good Friend' would:

- Demonstrate being trustworthy.
- Give space to others if they need it.
- Show concern for another person's happiness.
- Believe in the best of the other person.
- Know someone's weaknesses but don't point them out.
- Always look forward to spending time together.
- Cry and laugh together.
- Share honesty and sensitivity
- Pray with them.
- Praise their strengths.

You have to play it by ear for your particular circumstance, but you do have to deal with it, address it, and move on. Remember, communication requires listening also. Your perception may not have been the intent. So do as much listening as you do talking when facing the other person. You may never forget about it, but you have to forgive in order to move forward.

Laugh when you can, apologize when you should and let go of what you cannot change

How to Develop the Courage to Do What You Thought You Couldn't

You can do anything. Yes, you can do anything! You can do anything you set your mind to do. If you think you can't, then you lack courage.

We are all born without fear and have the courage to do anything. That's right; no fear. Just watch babies. They put anything in their mouths, they touch anything, and they have a fear of nothing. Fear is a learned behavior. We learn to become afraid as we experiment while growing. Courage is a learned behavior also. It's something we put into our minds that enables us to face things without feeling inhibited.

Most people treat courage like fear and give up once they've failed one time. Courage, however, is part of our integrity. Courage is what makes us who we are; it's part of our credibility as a person.

Having courage is only having the confidence and control of you mind by being able to face your fears. You may at the time appear to be brave but in reality, you have stepped beyond your weaknesses and controlled your them with your belief in yourself.

Working through fears, weaknesses and intimidations result in your growth in life.

- You lead as you would like to be led.
- You have developed commitment.
- You are focused on your strengths and not your weaknesses.
- You show a passion to service others.
- You show integrity.
- You think through before you act.
- You are open to learning new things without fear.
- You are open to new tasks.

Understand that you can do anything you want, but you must believe in yourself, build your character, and have the courage to develop the qualities for your integrity.

Believe you can, and you're halfway there.

As children we learned that courage is the ability to face our fears. Courage is the quality in your mind that enables you to face your fears with confidence and take firm control of yourself.

If you're afraid of water, you control your mind to face your fear of water with confidence and a firm control of yourself to push through it. The same use of mind control/courage is used for overcoming the fear of insects, animals, darkness, crowds, crossing a bridge, and so on. Does it work? That depends on the person and the mind over matter ability they have to retrain their own brain.

I'm afraid of spiders, roaches and flying. To overcome my fear, I learned to handle my mind control/courage by getting angry at the spider or roach and telling it off—"Get out of my house! You don't come in my house!"—before I dispose of it. As a child, that is how I learned to get my firm control with confidence. It's worked since—mind over matter. I overcame my greatest fear of flying, by taking flying lessons in a program that had you up in the plane and in the air more than on the ground in the classroom.

So if courage originates from mind control, then why do many people have difficulty controlling their emotions, knowing right from wrong, honesty, making sacrifices, taking risks, sharing, or controlling pain, among so many other things? It might be that these things are more emotional. Although they're also controlled by our minds, we seem to find it easier to have courage to overcome the visible fears. Our emotional fears? Not so much control there.

Here are some actions take courage many would have trouble handling:

- starting a conversation with someone you do not know.
- admitting you are wrong outload to someone.
- telling the truth even if it means losing friends.
- doing what is right in your heart when others do not agree.
- saying no when you do not believe something is right.
- defending someone who is considered unpopular.
- giving something your very best, regardless of pain or discomfort.
- be willing to take a risk.
- being the only one who believes something can be done.

- confronting your fears without running away from them.
- be willing to go first.
- being honest about your fears, and failures.
- believing in your faith with all your heart, regardless of the cost.
- sacrifice yourself to protect someone you love, or someone wronged.

The next time you come across something or are confronted with admitting or risking something, take action that takes courage.

"Change your thoughts, and you change your world."
—Norman Vincent Peale

Looking at Hope

Everyone seems to always have hope—I hope it doesn't rain, I hope we eat soon because I'm hungry, I hope my hair looks good—but that's not what I had in mind. Hope is merely something we wish for or for which we have expectations. Or are you just looking for four-leaf clovers? Many people live their days by hoping for something. What happens if you don't get what you hope for? Are you just gambling, throwing the dice to see if it's your lucky day?

I have a simple message regarding hope.

- Hope opens doors, where despair closes them.
- Hope looks for the good in people, instead of harping on the worst in them.
- Hope discovers what can be done, instead of grumbling about what cannot be done.
- Hope lights a candle, instead of cursing the darkness.
- Hope draws its power from a deep trust in God and the basic goodness of humankind.
- Hope regards problems, small or large, as opportunities.
- Hope cherishes no illusions, nor does it give way to skepticism.

Have a different perspective on things, and don't just go through life hoping for things to happen your way. Embrace the opportunities that come your way instead of using your hope to bring you things that are not meant to happen.

Instead, BELIEVE in yourself, that you have within yourself the best will happen for you, no matter what.

Believe in the person you want to become

CHAPTER 10

LOSS

Facing a sudden or unexpected loss is never easy, nor gathering yourself to deal with it. There are as many ways to deal with a loss as there are people in this world, but the key is to remember there is never a right or a wrong way to do it. There is only your own way that is within your own heart. The amount of time spent grieving also varies and should never be measured. This chapter on loss is so important to understand. There is no "one size fits all" for this issue. You must do it your way, just yours. This chapter will give you thoughts and situations to take ideas from. How you handle loss is up to you.

How to Guide a Child Who Is Grieving from a Loss

Death and dying are difficult enough for adults to manage and understand, but children have a particularly hard time. They often don't understand the concept of death, and experiencing a loss at a young age can alter their lives forever. When children face the death of a relative, parent, friend, or pet, they need proper support. This often begins when they first learn of a terminal diagnosis.

This sensitive subject should be handled carefully. Children know more than you think, but they also have vivid imaginations if they don't have the answers to something confusing. If you are grieving, they may not to ask questions because they see you're upset.

Children also are more apt to blame themselves for someone's getting sick or dying. His is also true when a pet dies. They'll feel if they hadn't said or done something, the person or pet wouldn't have died. Also, if someone is in the hospital, children tend to view a hospital as a place to die and will reject any future suggestions of going to the hospital to visit anyone. Children's minds work by association. They think their presence or activities may have been the cause of someone's loss of life. The child's mind and must be taken into consideration.

There are ways, however, you can help a child who is grieving. Remember the loss of a person or a pet are equally devastating and confusing, and each hurt tremendously.

How to Guide Children Who Are Grieving a Loss

Be honest. Even while you are grieving, children look to you for hope and encouragement. When they ask questions, avoid giving them a pat response. Admit you don't have all the answers.

Give them opportunities for creative expression. When children have difficulty verbalizing their feelings, it may be easier for them to express them on paper. Drawing is an effective way for children to gain control over their emotional pain and gradually reduce that pain.

Encourage children to continue with their normal family routines. Maintain and provide security by letting children know there are certain constants in their lives and things they can rely on that stay the same.

Give children permission to grieve. Regardless of the type of loss, your children need permission to mourn. They need to hear from you that it's okay to be sad.

Watch your expectations. Be careful not to overprotect you children. Lecturing or making decisions for them is not helpful while they're coping with a loss. Don't take that power and ability away from them to make decisions. Lecturing is not what their minds need when they're already overloaded by grieving.

Allow your children to respond in their own way. Don't expect children to respond as you do. If they begin to express strong feelings, don't block them. Allow them to cry and express anger or bitterness.

Create opportunities for play. Periodically your children may need to be encouraged to take a break from their grief to play with their friends. Playing helps children regain a feeling of safety and security.

Be available when your children are grieving—this may be the most important element in helping your children to grieve. Remember they need affection and a sense of security.

Remember how important pet grieving is. Never call a pet "just" a dog, turtle, cat, or hamster. These companions were their best friends, their buddies, their sleep mates, their siblings, their family. Don't minimize the importance of a pet that means the world to your children.

You have a responsibility to guide your children in understanding and coping with grief.

Never look at children as not being part of the grieving process. They have the disadvantage of not understanding or not having the facts as adult do, but their grief is just as real as yours.

Be there for them as you would for your own mate. Guiding children through the grieving process is a teachable moment for both of you.

Pain is inevitable. Suffering is optional.

Quick Reference Guide through Grief

You never expected this. What just happened? No, this can't be.

Whether it was an expected passing after an illness or sudden and unexpected, no one is ever prepared for losing a loved one. Regardless of whether it was your husband, wife, partner, child, parent, sibling, or friend, the pain, ache, confusion, fog, and lack of direction is still the same hollow feeling. If you have gone through this incredible loss, I am so very sorry and truly ache for you.

There is no other pain in the world that even comes close to losing someone you love and care about. I've been through it. I've lived it. I've not gotten over it either. But I have learned how to cope with it, and you will too, eventually, in your own time. Our devastating experiences, however, don't align closely enough to compare because we are each different. What helped me may not help you.

I can, however, share a few general thoughts I have shared with patients' loved ones. I hope these will help you to work through your own situation.

- Lean into your pain.
- Pace yourself.
- Welcome help from those who love you.
- Look beyond people's words.
- Protect your physical health.
- Be prepared and ready for a second wave of grief.
- Trust the recovery process.
- Refuse to live with regrets.
- Avoid major changes.
- Let your grief benefit others.

Remember that no two people grieve or handle things the same way. You have to do what's best for you.

You will get through this, but there is no time frame, no countdown clock. *Do not* be in a hurry to get back to being busy, that's not recommended for anyone.

> *I am blessed with an incredible family and wonderful friends.*

Why Am I Still Grieving?

Have you found yourself saying, "I know he's gone," or "I know she's in a better place. It's been a long time now, but why am I still grieving?"

Losing someone who meant the world to you—the love of your life, best friend, and soul mate—is a pain and emptiness that never seems to leave you. You may say, "It's been a while now, but I just can't move. I see others doing things and laughing, and it seems like they forgot already. What's wrong with them? What's wrong with *me?*" The answer is, nothing is wrong with anyone. Grief has no time limit and is entirely different for everyone. You cannot rush through grief, you cannot omit grief, you cannot delay grief, you cannot deny grief. At some point whether immediately or 1, 2, 5 10 years from someone's death who had a large space in your heart, it will hit you without warning.

After the loss of a loved one, there are also other types of those wrenching feelings which are something others don't understand unless they've been through it. If it's been a year, however, or five or ten years or more, and you're still grieving, then you may be stuck.

Being stuck is very unpleasant; you see the world moving on, your family and friends are growing, everyone else's life is different now, but you're still aching for and grieving the loss of your loved one, your world, your life mate. Removing yourself from being stuck is something only you can do because you are the only one who understands and feels the pain. You are the only source that can transition yourself to feeling and moving forward.

First, understand that moving forward does not mean you're walking away from your deceased mate. It does not disrespect him or her or what you had together. It does not cause you to forget him or her. Moving forward helps you to embrace your blessed life with your loved one and to feel honored to have shared a love like you had. It's humbling to realize that someone cared enough about you to have dedicated himself or herself to you. Moving forward gives you the transition that you need to live in the present.

Please consider the following ways to stop grieving and start living:

Remember that remaining distraught for a long period of time is not proof that you "really loved" someone. There's no disputing that; if you hadn't really loved the person, you wouldn't have felt the loss in the first place.

Healing is a testament to your recuperative powers, not condemnation for your inability to care.

When you become still, the pain may resurface. That's fine; let it be there, but continue your inner work of healing. Hurt that arises during prayer, meditation, or contemplation is healing in nature.

When praying, change the focus of your prayers. Instead of asking why, start a new prayer and ask primarily for the strength to endure, the power to heal, and the wisdom to learn.

Keep a journal. Putting your thoughts and emotions on paper is a good way to let things out and put them in order. Don't promise yourself you'll write every day. Journal writing is for when you feel the devastation and pain, and you need to "talk" on paper. Write whenever you feel like it, but do not let yourself feel guilty for not writing every day or even every week.

Let yourself heal fully until the process has run its course because the convalescence period is very important. If you don't allow the hurt to heal completely, you may find you are emotionally oversensitive. Let yourself heal.

Start to affirm yourself by making the firm, loving, healing, and positive thoughts come out about yourself and your life. An affirmation sends the message of yourself, the "I am" message. Claim what you want as though you already have it. "I am healthy. I am happy. I am making it. I am alive. I am surviving. I am healing fully. My heart is mending. I am stronger. I have the courage to grow. I am grateful for so much. I am a better person for having loved. I am always going to feel loved."

Colors can affect your spirit, mood, or your strength. You feel different walking into a dimly lit black room than you do walking into a brightly lit yellow room. As much as possible, stay in the "up" spectrum of colors—yellow, orange, red, and pastels. Surround yourself with greens—clothing, food, furniture, or plants. Green is soothing and seems to promote healing and growth. Try to stay away from black and blue; you've already been bruised enough.

Laugh! Laughter is one of the most healing activities. Whatever makes you laugh, just do it. Rent a video, buy a comedy tape, read a funny book, talk to people who make you laugh. Ask your friends to call you with anecdotes or jokes they may have. Yes, it's okay to laugh; even laugh about your loss. There's a fine line between tragedy and comedy. Seeing the humor in your loss, your reaction to the loss, and even your memories about what was lost can be healing. The loss is no less painful, and you're not being disrespected or disloyal by seeing the humor in things. In fact, humor and laughter can honor the relationship.

As you continue to heal, you'll find that your thinking sharpens, your judgment is sounder and more reliable, your concentration and memory improve, and you want to be around more people and do more for others. Your feelings will become more expansive, optimistic, and alive. You'll feel stronger, more content, and independent, and you'll want to get out, get moving, and try new things.

At a certain point, it's time to leave the loss behind and move on. Don't be surprised if you miss the process of mourning. Some people mourn the loss of the mourning process. Let go of the past, look forward to the future, and keep moving ahead. Let yourself enjoy the excitement of uncertainty.

Remember, others may still be morning too. They may be grieving the loss of your loved one but also may be mourning you. They've lost you too because you are still mourning and are not the same person they knew and loved. They are mourning that loss and change in you. Reach out to them and help them.

Take stock of the good. The relationship brought you a great deal of good, which is why you miss it so terribly. Know that much of it is still with you. Now is the time to remember the good—your loved one taught you to appreciate good food and develop interests in new things, new people, new clothing, or silly things that brought you laughter.

You are a better person for having loved. You cared, you became involved, you learned to invest in yourself, and your interaction permitted loving and caring. Even though you lost the love of your life, you are a better person for having loved and been loved.

You are a richer, deeper, wiser person for having invested in a relationship. Praise yourself for your courage in relating to others, to have had the ability to feel. Now it's time to learn from your loss and recognize what you can do with what you've learned.

Live your life and help others. Develop new interests in something you've never done—gardening, swimming, golf, reading, cooking, baking, knitting, tennis, canning, garment weaving, painting, aerobics. The world is your menu; select something that will challenge you. Try something, and exercise your mind and body.

Your happiness is up to you; moving forward is up to you. You are only given one life, and what you do with it is up to you. Not moving forward, however, is not an option.

Choose moving forward, choose living, choose being happy and loving your life. The individual you lost would not approve of your being stuck. He or she would want you to move forward, feeling blessed with what you had together. It's really okay to just let go.

Sometimes you have to let go to allow new things to come into your life.

How Are You Handling Your Loss?

life still seem to be nothing but daily hurdles you're forced to jump over again and again?

Handling heartbreaking losses, dealing with life changes, losing your job, losing your best friend is never, never easy. That constant fog is still there. Will you get over it? No, you won't, but you will eventually learn to get through one day at a time.

In my long career in nursing, I've seen some of the most horrific sudden losses as well as the expected end of a long battle. It's always the same devastating feeling for those left behind.

Then the question is, "Now what?" Moving forward after a loss almost seems disrespectful to the one who's gone. Moving forward—or even living—sometimes seems like an act of not caring that the loved one is gone. Picking yourself back up from such a devastating loss is something you will have to make yourself do. Your best friend can't help you; your family can't help you; no one can, It has to be you. It's not disrespectful; it's responsible for you to get up.

Here are suggestions for getting past your devastation and sadness after a loss of any kind. First, give yourself time to grieve; then, try these:

Surround yourself with positives. Fill your life with positive people, positive music, positive books, and positive situations. Stay away from negatives—sad music, TV, movies, or news. Positives make you feel better, and as you feel better, you begin to lose that feeling of being so down and depressed.

Be active. Physical activity can lift you out of your sad feelings. Enjoy the outdoors, especially when it's sunny. If your garden only reminds you of who you just lost, dig in and keep it going, but add your own items and variations to give that garden your style and taste. Then you won't start creating a shrine to the loved one, which can happen if you don't change it up and add your own personality to the mix. Activity energizes your mind and causes it to secrete healthy endorphins that will assist in your healing.

Eat healthy. Pay attention to this, even if you don't want to hear it: eat plenty of fruits and vegetables. Avoid caffeine, sugar, junk food, and alcohol. Why? Fruits and vegetables have natural sugars, as well as other minerals in them, and they have no caffeine or depressants. Fruits and vegetables work to boost your body and mind by also keeping your blood sugar at a regular level. Sharp jumps and drops in your blood sugar are due to all the added sugars and caffeine; alcohol acts as depressant.

Get enough sleep. Exhaustion adds to depression. Sleep refreshes the body, uplifts the spirit, and aids in energy, both physically and emotional, for you to handle daily issues. Avoid too much sleep, however, as this is a sign of avoiding important issues that can lead to your becoming depressed. If you're just too exhausted and need more sleep, you might need more positives in your life, more activity, and healthy food.

Write out your feelings. Keeping a journal is cathartic and will help you to cope with your loss.

Getting through the devastation of the loss of a loved one is best accomplished in small step and without rushing. Just remember to keep an open mind, be positive, and get through each day, one day at a time.

You must take control of your feelings before they take control of you.

What Are You Doing with Your Depression, Grief, and Discouragement?

When your life changes suddenly due to the traumatic loss of a loved one, a financial loss, loss of a job, loss of your home or car, an accident, or an ongoing parade of challenges and obstacles, what are you doing about it? Simply ignoring it will not make it go away. You must face it and deal with it.

Start with the following three steps:

1. alone time
2. consoling and listening time
3. absorbing the reality/alone time

After you've had time to be alone, listen, and absorb what's happened, then you can start another phase. There's a lot in your head, and much is still foggy. But now you need to write out your feelings. Emotions trapped inside of you only increase depression. Getting them out on paper can release the internal pressure. Write about your anger, grief, confusion, loss, stress, emptiness, what to do, pain, and anything else that's bothering you.

Be very honest and elaborate as much as you like, but get it out on paper. Then fold it and put it away somewhere—and don't look at it again. This is part of the process of getting back up, moving forward, and getting control of yourself again.

Tragedies do not come with instructions on what to do next, but because I've gone through this, I'm giving you the instructions. One year after you put away the paper with your thoughts and feelings written on it, get it and read what you wrote down. This will help you to realize how far you have come in that year of enormous grief, pain, and despair.

The only way you are going to believe how far you have come from your tragedy is to see it in your writing. It won't take you back and ruin any progress you've made. Instead, your note will be your confirmation and affirmation of what you have accomplished.

My friend, you have to believe that you can do it. No one else can possibly do this for you. You can, you will, you have. Hang on to this belief, and you'll be on your way.

Accept what is, let go of what was, and have faith in what will be.

Has Grief Taken Over Your Life?

Loss hurts

If you have been lost someone very special to you, I am truly sorry for that loss. My thoughts and prayers are surrounding you right now. Even those of us who have gone through a loss don't know what you are going through within your own feelings. We can imagine because we went through it ourselves, and it was terrible; it hurts, it's heartbreaking, it's awful. But knowing someone's deep feelings is not a skill any of us has.

We may tell people, "I know what you're going through"; "I understand how you feel"; "I know the pain you feel"; "You'll get through this"; "You're strong"; or "It's for the best."

Think before you use one of those phrases because they are truly empty words for person you are trying to console. The person is still numb and in the "why did this happen?" phase.

I'm sharing the following little nuggets of direction to cope with grief. Use them when you're ready.

- Take time and pace yourself.
- Push through the pain. It's hard, but don't let it consume you.
- There will be a second wave of grief, but you're not regressing. It's part of the recovery.
- Trust the recovery process. Don't try to skip any stage or deny it because you breathe without awareness, and the grief process happens without awareness.
- Welcome help from those you love and trust. Don't push away people; these are the people with whom you can be yourself and they understand.
- Take care of your physical health. Not eating or sleeping isn't going to give you the strength to get through this loss.
- Do not live in regret! Living with "would have, should have, why didn't I?" is gone. Live moving forward, and let it go.

- This is not the time for major changes. Don't make major housing, employment, or business changes now. Let things settle.
- Don't let yourself take people's words as the gospel. You need to look beyond their words and advice until your fog clears.
- Let your grief benefit others. Everyone who's trying to console you is also grieving; share together and support each other during this time.

How do you know if you are recovering and have turned the corner? And should you feel guilty when you do? No, don't feel guilty about moving forward; it doesn't mean you've forgotten about the loved one; he or she is still in your heart. You'll know, however, that you're coming back to yourself when:

- you start taking care of yourself, and it's not only okay but feels good
- you start to get through those special days without falling apart
- doing things for yourself is not so scary
- you find yourself reaching out to others when they're going through a loss or disappointment
- your emotional ups and downs start becoming less and less often, and when they occur, you pull yourself through them
- you realize you forgot to visit the cemetery or do a special ritual you had, and you forgot without grief. It's okay; you're moving on.

Grief can be tremendous and powerful, but you must have the strength within yourself to push beyond the pain and keep moving forward. You may think you need to start over, but that's not so. You need to move on, move forward, and keep going.

Start your life where you are at this moment. Use your strength and your skills. Do what you can, one day at a time.

Again, my thoughts and prayers are with you now.

CHAPTER 11

Medical and Health

This chapter is special to me as a nurse, but I can only share reality with you, not medical advice. I can show you how this information, when used correctly, can affect how you handle your health and how these issues can suddenly affect your mind. The categories in this chapter are the largest issues that affect our minds and bodies. I hope you learn something helpful that may guide you in the future.

"What Do You Mean I Have Cancer?"

The scariest three words you will ever hear are "You have cancer." So many men, women, and children have been told those ugly three words. Hearing that diagnosis is stressful, but being told "you have cancer" is a whole different kind of stress than daily stress.

I've heard hundreds of patients receive this news, but one was more devastating than all the others. I was sitting in the doctor's office with my father and mother when the doctor came in and told my dad, "You have cancer." The shock of hearing those three words is unbelievable.

Patients who'd received this news often looked at me for supportive answers, but I could only hug them and start the next steps of what was coming, the treatments they'd have, and the specific information about their diagnosis. I'd reassure them they were not alone and would give the numbers to call for support. They needed answers, and but they wouldn't know what questions to ask until later, after the news sank in. I was their resource and had to be ready when they were ready to talk.

My own father looked at me the minute he was told "you have cancer," and I knew he wanted me to give him supportive answers. I was in disbelief as much as he was, but I could be was his ears to hear the rest of the information—the treatments, the schedules, the time left for him, and everything else that's discussed.

My dad needed me, just as all of those patients did. He needed answers, and as with the other patients, I knew Mom and Dad wouldn't have questions until later. I was their resource. I knew they weren't ready to talk, but eventually they would need information.

My dad was a very private man. He kept to himself, didn't express negatives or disappointments, and stayed positive for everyone all the time. But this three-word bullet he received went right through him in a way nothing had before.

Hearing those three words does something to you that many don't understand until they have heard the words themselves. At one of my own doctor's visits, I was waiting for results of the annual tests that were done. I'd thought about canceling the appointment because my results were always the same thing—I was fit, in great health, and had boundless energy—and I had a lot of errands to do by five o'clock that day. As I was mentally going over my to-do list, the doctor came in and sat down. I assumed he was going to give me my usual "you're in good shape; keep it up" speech. I thought, *Man I should have just canceled this appointment and saved the co-pay for groceries. This has already taken too long, and I've got to go!*

Instead of giving me a glowing report, however, he said, "You have cancer."

I was still thinking about my busy day and my to-do list getting bigger, and I didn't catch what he said. "What? I'm sorry; I was distracted."

He looked in my eyes and repeated, "Linda, you have cancer—breast cancer."

When I heard the words I became frozen, went numb, and never heard another thing he said. I saw his mouth moving. He gave me a hug, but I felt nothing. I heard nothing. He spoke for some time, but I heard nothing. Instead, I heard the words, "Linda, you have cancer—breast cancer," over and over and over. I never realized he'd left the room. I didn't see or hear a nurse come in later. I didn't know, see, hear, or feel anything. I was completely numb. I had no idea I was breathing.

I cannot tell you how long I sat there. I don't remember being helped to the front desk, or even getting up and being given appointments for surgery scheduled in forty-eight hours, treatment schedules, medications/prescriptions, procedure instructions, times, places, papers, new doctors' names and words, oncologists, surgeons, Cancer Center, instructions—nothing. It was and still is a blank.

I thought of so many of my patients being told this. I thought of my dad being told this. I thought about so many things that didn't make sense. Who was with me? No one; just the doctor and me. Did anyone hear what was said? No one; just the doctor and me.

The following morning, I got up and felt exhausted by this horrible dream I'd just had that seemed so real, but I was so happy it was just a dream and tried to shake it off. I went downstairs to start coffee and get ready for work. I walked past the kitchen table and saw crinkly papers laying there. I picked them up and quickly realized that I hadn't had a dream; it was real Then I heard the doctor's voice: "Linda, you have cancer—breast cancer."

I spun around because I thought he was behind me; it sounded so loud and clear, but there wasn't anyone there. I looked at the papers again and saw the diagnosis: breast cancer.

I dropped to my knees on the floor. *This is real. This is me. How can this happen? No, it can't be true. It was a terrible dream.* I looked at the papers again—diagnosis: breast cancer.

When I'd left the doctor's office the day before after I received my diagnosis and felt numb and frozen, I had no further recollection of anything that happened after that. Nothing. Although I'd driven to the doctor's office to the other side of town, when I left the doctor's office with all those papers and instructions, I left the building and walked all the way home. I never went to my car. I never thought anything except those words: "Linda, you have cancer—breast cancer."

I don't remember walking home or how I got there. I remember nothing but those three words: you have cancer.

But I have to work. I have to get to the ER. They're expecting me—my patients, the traumas that are coming in. Wait, what's happening?

Then I heard him again: "Linda, you have cancer—breast cancer."

I remained numb and frozen in time, and to this day I have no idea how long I was like that. From the looks of the house, I didn't eat; I didn't do anything but sit in that chair and then went to bed with my clothes from yesterday still on. The papers on the table appeared wrinkled on one side from clutching them in my hand on the walk home.

So why am I talking about my cancer today and parallel stress with it? This isn't about me or my cancer. This is about everyone who has ever received those horrific three words: "You have cancer." The stress of receiving a cancer diagnosis and the state of mind that you're put into is like nothing you've ever felt in your life. From that moment on, you hear nothing else, little things don't matter anymore; they're trivial and foolish.

The stress of receiving a cancer diagnosis puts you in a state of survival, a body and soul fight. Once you have your head wrapped around this thing, it's an internal battle of survival. A cancer diagnosis causes a "no, no, no, not now. I'm not ready. I can't. Not now, no." It cannot happen to me" … but it did.

The stress of cancer is a stress battle of survival—not traffic, not deadlines, not work, not gossip, not hurt feelings, not burned dinner, not a mess on the floor. The stress you have with cancer is a battle stress of survival, damn it! Why? Because you have to. You have to do it. You have to go through it. You must do it yourself, for you and not for anyone else but you. No one can get you through this, but you.

Cancer must be looked at, not as stress; but a mission, a job that you work at every day, nonstop. You never quit, you never stop thinking about it, and you never give up!

For those who have been through cancer and lost, my heart goes out to their families and friends. My thoughts and prayers are with you because you're right; it isn't fair.

God bless all the cancer survivors out there who have, like me, battled and won this thing and lived through those three scariest words: "You have cancer."

When you feel like you cannot go another step, that's when you give it everything you have got

This Is What You Don't Know about Cancer

This is a touchy subject that most do not want to talk about. It's the most foul, unforgiven, and feared six-letter word in the world. Many of us have lost family, friends, and loved ones to this evil disease, or you may be going through this hell yourself. As I've mentioned, the greatest man I know, my father, died of cancer. He too heard and endured that horrible 6 letter word bolt right through him. However, there are also those who have been blessed to have recovered from cancer and I applaud them.

As I've mentioned, when I heard my diagnosis, all I heard was the word *cancer* and absolutely nothing else. I shut off all sounds around me. Like many of you, I saw the doctor's lips moving, but I heard nothing but the word cancer. It repeated over and over and over again in my head, sort of like a song you can't get out of your mind. The word—cancer, cancer, cancer—was deafening. When I received my diagnosis, I was divorced and living in another state from my family, whom I knew had their plates completely full themselves. My parents had already passed. I was in complete shock for a while, like everyone who gets that diagnosis, that sentence. However, I foolishly kept the entire diagnosis and occurrence to myself. In fact, I never told anyone for over 10 years because I was afraid. I was afraid if I spoke of it before 10 years had past long behind me, it may return, like my Dad's did on his 10 year anniversary of having it initially removed. As a nurse, I knew this was stupid, but as a daughter I didn't, it was still very vivid within my mind and my heart. So I told no one.

I should have expected it, I guess. My mother had breast cancer when I was four years old, but with immediate care, surgery, and treatments, she was a survivor.

As a nurse; I should have been better prepared to handle it. I was not. I went through the surgeries, the treatments, and the continuous doctor's and testing appointments. This was a new way of life, and it was ongoing. It's a special club that we have. No one is ever prepared to handle cancer. That diagnosis pulls you into a cave of dark, unknown areas. You hear, but you don't comprehend.

For anyone who has been blown apart in some way by this six-letter word—whether it was your diagnosis or someone you know—I want to tell you what you might not know about cancer. This is what cancer *cannot* do:

- It cannot silence courage.
- It cannot kill friendship.
- It cannot corrode faith.
- It cannot destroy peace.
- It cannot shatter hope.
- It cannot cripple love.
- It cannot suppress memories.
- It cannot invade the soul.
- It cannot conquer the spirit.
- It cannot steal eternal life.

Cancer is limited in these areas. It cannot touch our love, hope, faith, peace, friendships, memories, or courage. It cannot touch our souls, spirits, or eternal lives. Why? Because we are strong, we believe, we are supportive, we live in the moment and we have patience.

When you see us, we want no special treatment; we are no different from you. We just want to be loved, as always. The only difference between you and someone who has or had cancer is that cancer survivors are stronger. We love more, we cherish longer, and we give more frequently. Bless all of you survivors and fighters. God Speed.

Accept what is, let go of what was, and have faith in what will be.

How You Can Avoid Hurting Your Back

"Oh, my back hurts!" I hear this all the time. The patients come in and the staff comes to work with the "oh my back hurts" complaints. We all hear warnings of what to do and not do to prevent back pain, but apparently few are listening. I'll share some ideas, though, so you don't have to say, "Oh, my back hurts."

Here's how to avoid hurting your back:

- Sit down to put on your socks, shoes, and pants; do not bend over to do that.
- Lift heavy objects no higher than your waist.
- Avoid lying or sleeping on your stomach.
- Bend at your hips, not at your waist.
- Get down on one knee before picking up a small child or infant from the floor.
- When reading, don't bend your neck and shoulders; bring the book up to your eyes. Place whatever you're reading on two pillows on your lap and prop the reading material on top of them.

Your back and back muscles carry most of the weight of your body. If you strain your back muscles because you are not properly using your back, your back's will hurt.

If you have chronic back pain without an old fracture injury or disc or vertebrae issue, check your posture and the list above. If you still have chronic back pain, and you are doing the proper things from the above list, check your scale. Being overweight puts too much pressure on your back. Those excess pounds may be too much.

This can also be said about chronic knee pain. Don't abuse your body; you need every bit of it. Take the time to use good body mechanics, and don't be in such a hurry. You'll hurt something else.

Getting Enough Sleep?

I'm pretty sure most of us would say we *do not* get enough sleep. Think about how you feel when you're awake. Have you had a few rough times just making it through the day? Do you spend your days off trying to catch up on sleep? Let me be clear: you cannot "catch up" on sleep. Once it's gone, it's gone. The best you can do is take it easier for the next couple of days.

Look at the following statements and see which of these pertain to you:

1. I have to use an alarm clock to wake me at a certain time.
2. It's a struggle to get out of bed in the morning.
3. I always feel like I need to get more sleep.
4. I feel tired, irritable, and stressed out during the workweek.
5. I have trouble concentrating and remembering.
6. I feel slow in critical thinking skills, problem solving, and being creative.
7. I fall asleep often while watching television.
8. I fall asleep often in meetings, lectures, or in warm rooms.
9. I frequently fall asleep after heavy meals or after a small amount of alcohol.
10. I often fall asleep while relaxing after dinner.
11. I often fall asleep within five minutes of getting into bed.
12. I frequently feel drowsy while driving.
13. I often need a nap to get through the day.
14. I often sleep extra hours on weekends.
15. I have dark circles around or under my eyes.

If you answered yes to three or more of those statements, you probably are not getting enough sleep.

Unfortunately, you are not alone. Even if you are not working, or you work for yourself and set your own hours, you still may need more sleep. Stress can make you edgy and can drain your system of rest. Another sleep or rest drainer is feeling bad about yourself or your circumstances. Feeling down is like stress and zaps all your energy.

Now what? What can you do?

First, change your sleep patterns. Go to bed earlier. Give yourself thirty more minutes to sleep. Don't over exert yourself during the day. Take it easy.

If you've tried going to bed earlier or have tried other methods to help you sleep for more than three weeks, it's time to get help. Your physician can help get you back on track, but you must be honest about what's going on in your life. This is critical in determining what's causing your fatigue, as many factors can cause sleep deprivation. These could include physical issues that are worth checking out. It could be that you hate your job or have problems at home, financial problems, or emotional issues. Consulting your physician or practitioner is the best way to resolve this.

Take care of this lack-of-sleep issue before it affects you physically or emotionally. Remember your body is an incredible machine, but it's also very sensitive. Fix the problem before the problem fixes you.

Busy is a choice, stress is a choice, and joy is a choice.
Do something about your choices.

What Do You Mean I Might Die?

It was May 11, an incredibly beautiful sunny day, with the temperature in the mid-seventies. It was one of those stunningly clear, bright days when you just want to play hooky and sit on a bench by a lake in the shade of a tree with a glass of iced tea and a good book. I woke with a burst of energy, but the only thing I had to do on this day was go to my doctor's appointment to get the test results from my new patient exam.

My dog, Lacey, and I lost track of time as we walked on the lakeshore and watched the ducks and boats. Suddenly, Lacey got too close to the edge of the pier and fell into the lake, but she started instinctively swimming, even though that was her first time in the water. I pulled her out quickly, but that slip into the lake scared her from going back in willingly. We resumed our walk along the lakeshore.

I looked at the clock on my phone and realized I needed to get Lacey home so I could get to my doctor's appointment on time. I didn't think my appointment would take very long, so I thought that maybe we could walk to Dairy Queen for some ice cream after I got back from my appointment. It would be really nice to introduce Lacey to her first ice cream treat.

I had recently rescued Lacey from the county shelter. It had been two years since Lexie died, and I realized it was time to start looking for another fur buddy. When I walked in the shelter, they pointed to the door for dogs and invited me to look around as long as I wanted. It seemed that every dog in there was barking to plead his or her personal case. It was very cool in there—it was January—and the scent of wet dog just seemed to give that extra chill of nervousness. I realized that I was the one who was nervous. I almost felt like I was cheating on Lexie, who had died of respiratory complications after a long illness.

I made my way around the dog kennels, starting with the littlest ones and moving to the "big dog" room. The big dogs were medium-sized and larger; I could hear the difference as their barking went from yips to deep barks. Every dog in that place seemed to be barking except for one, a mostly white, long haired, medium-sized dog that just lay in her cage. Her name tag on the cage door read "Fluffy," but I didn't think that name suited her. She was just too big to be a Fluffy. Fluffy is a miniature poodle-size dog, not this big dog. I was undecided, so I left to think about it.

Back at home, I couldn't stop thinking about Fluffy. I looked up her picture and profile on the shelter's website. She was a mix of border collie and Akita. When I inquired about her, they told me she was deaf and that four different families had taken her home, but all had brought her back. No one wanted Fluffy; they said she didn't get along with children or she didn't handle well on a leash—and she was deaf. I went back to see her again, and she was still the only dog in the place not barking. I used my hands to signal to her, asking if she wanted to come home with me, and she immediately stood up and came to the gate. I took her home.

I read all her papers from the shelter to find out more about her. She had lived most of her two and a half years in a shelter and spent her earliest years in a high-kill shelter in Kentucky before being shipped to my local shelter. I changed her name to Lacey after getting a lot of suggestions from friends. She is the most loving, smartest, easiest to handle, and *not* deaf dog I've ever had. She makes my heart smile every day and is so joyful and fun to be with as she discovers new experiences, like ice cream and the lake!

Lives can change in an instant

As I walked into the clinic for my doctor's appointment, and while in the lobby I saw an older woman come out of the doctor's office. She was frail and pale, and her eyes were so sad, but she remained quiet as she waited for her paperwork. She sat down across from me. After a couple of moments, she looked up and met my gaze. I smiled at her and noticed her eyes welled up with tears. She looked down and began fidgeting with her hands. I realized she likely had been given a sad diagnosis, and my heart went out to her.

In my long career as an RN, I witnessed countless people receive sad diagnoses. As their nurse, I was able to give them the compassion they required. However, in the case of this poor frail lady sitting across from me, I was in an uncomfortably foreign position. She was not my patient, and I was not her nurse. I stared down at the magazine in my hands, thinking that she shouldn't be alone at this time. Suddenly, I heard a voice saying something to me and realized the sad lady was speaking to me. "I'm so sorry, dear. Thank you for your sweet smile."

I smiled again and thanked her.

"Are you here to see the doctor, or waiting for someone?" she asked.

"I'm seeing the doctor," I said.

"He's such a good man and a good doctor."

Most patients don't compliment a doctor who has given them a sad diagnosis. *I must have been wrong about her situation*, I thought.

After several long minutes, she said quietly, "He gave me some bad news."

I looked up, and she was looking right at me. Without hesitation, I asked, if she was alright, is there anything I could do …

She nodded, saying, "Would you mind?"

As I took the seat next to her, I saw her eyes were tearing up. I took her pale, slender hand into mine. "What can I do to help?" I asked.

"I'm all alone, and I've been given bad news."

"Is there anyone I could call for you?"

She nodded and said, "My daughter."

She gave me her daughter's number I moved to a spot closer to the windows where I could get better reception on my cell phone. I called her daughter immediately and informed her that her mother would like her to come to the doctor's office with, but I did not tell her the news her mother had been given.

As I came back to the older woman, I found her staring at the wall. I sat down beside her and again took her hand in mine and introduced myself again and said her daughter would be coming right over to be with her at the clinic.

She thanked me and told me her name was Maggie. "I just don't know what to do. I'm widowed, you know, and live alone. Now that nice doctor is telling me I may not live much longer. I just don't understand. How can that be when I feel fine? Now that I know, I just want to lie down and go to sleep.

I squeezed Maggie's hand gently and assured her the doctor must have a treatment plan for her he can review with them when her daughter arrives.

Maggie looked up at me with her eyes still teary saying "I'm just scared that I will die".

I pulled my chair around to face Maggie and softly said to her, "Maggie, only you have the power to believe in yourself. Only you have the strength to fight through this. Only you have to will to go on. Only you have the ability to believe in yourself. Your mind and your heart have to work together with these thoughts to get you through this. Don't give up; get strong. Don't give up; believe. Don't lie down; get up and fight. Your daughter will be here with you."

Maggie squeezed my hands, and a big smile spread across her face as she said, "I'm going to do that! I'm going to fight. I'm going to be strong, and I'm going to believe!" She then stood up, put her arms around my neck, and gave me a big hug.

At that moment, a woman approached us and I realized it was Maggie's daughter, "Lynn" as the frail woman had told me earlier. Then I was called into the doctor's office for my appointment, and as I turned to walk away, Maggie grabbed my arm, gave me another hug, and said "Thank you, dear. I'll never forget your words."

While sitting in the exam room, waiting for my test results, I smiled as I thought about Maggie. My doctor came in, and because we had worked together in the past, he gave me a big hug.

Doc (as I always call him) sat down on the stool, opened up his laptop and looked at me, saying, "I'm going to get right to this. You have bone cancer."

As I sat there looking at him, all I could hear was those two words: "bone cancer." I thought back to the year that my father had died from bone cancer, and all the patients I'd cared for who had received the diagnosis of bone cancer. I knew the drill— I had already been through this hearing that 6 letter word myself when I was diagnosed with Breast Cancer; the chemo treatments, the surgeries—but then there was the pain from bone cancer. It's the worst cancer pain there is. *My parents, friends, Lacey, my family, my nursing career, patients I've counseled, my book to be published, golf, Maggie*—all these thoughts raced through my head like a Formula One racer going 200 miles per hour, and the words *bone cancer* kept echoing over and over and over, again.

In the echoing, I heard Doc calling my name. He was looking at me and talking, but again I heard nothing—until I felt someone hug me. Doc and his nurse, a colleague of mine, were talking to me. Suddenly, my thoughts just stopped.

I looked at Doc and said, "No! This can't be. I don't feel like I have cancer. No, I don't."

Doc promised he was going to be with me through "the whole thing." I believed him because he was a unique physician, and I trusted him. He showed me the computer results and concerns from my initial visit with him two days earlier. He said, "We'll start running tests today, especially because of your breast cancer history."

Testing ran daily between lab work, imaging, and invasive scans, bone biopsy. It was a long week of getting poked and viewed inside and out, but it was necessary. I remained strong and confident that I was fine. The next Monday I was called back into Doc's office for results—but the results were inconclusive. So it was time for an oncology consult that would determine the source of the bone cancer. Doc called the oncologist, and they discussed the tests, lab work, and imaging, as well as making arrangements for me to see the oncologist the next day.

I'd initially kept the preliminary diagnosis and testing to myself, but I needed to inform my family. My brother knew what our dad had gone through, and it wouldn't have been fair to keep this from him. I'm very glad I did share this heavy load because I remembered only too well how hard it was handling this alone during my breast cancer many years ago.

The oncologist was from the United Kingdom, listening to his heavy UK accent brought me comfort; I have many wonderful online friends from the UK.

He reviewed my tests with me and showed me details on the computer and the plan he had for determining a correct diagnosis or ruling it out. It would start with more lab work. In addition, he ordered even more imaging and scheduled a bone biopsy procedure for me three days later. My results appointment was already scheduled for the following week. So I had seven full days to distract myself, keep up others' spirits, and wait for the results.

On June 16, 2016, I went in for my follow-up results appointment with my oncologist. He walked in the exam room and said, "You're fine. I do *not* believe this is cancer." And then he gave me a big hug. He said that through all my testing, they'd found out how incredibly healthy I really am. Then he sat down with his computer and said, "Let me show you this very rare type of bone condition you have." From that point forward, I had to force myself to concentrate on his words because all I could think about was how blessed I was to be cancer-free and healthy!

Driving home, I couldn't help but think about the nice older frail woman I met at the Clinic just week before. I couldn't stop smiling because when I'd spoken to her, I was helping her get back together in support of her sad diagnosis. At that moment when I was comforting her as a nurse, which I've done thousands of times with patients, I was giving her the words of strength, belief, and the will to get through her cancer diagnosis.

Little did I know at that time with that woman, that five minutes later, I too would have to put my mind and heart in sync to work together for the strength, belief, and will to get through my own cancer diagnosis for the next thirty-five days. Even as I shared my initial diagnosis with family and friends, I never told anyone that with bone cancer, one generally has, at best, six months to live. I never spoke those words to anyone because I never believed it in my heart or my mind.

It all begins and ends in your mind. What you give power to, has power over you, if you allow it

AFTERWORD

I would like to thank everyone who took the time to read this book. I hope you were able to take away something that helped you in your day.

As you have learned from this book, everything has meaning in your mind and everything you put into your mind will make a difference in how you handle everything else you are faced with in life.

BE sure you spend more time in choosing what you plant in your subconscious, there may be a time you will have to rely on your strength and beliefs. Let them be positive and enlightening for not only yourself, but for all those whom you cross paths with.

Many people have asked me how I got back up after where I've been, and where I'm going from here. I've explained the answer to the first question in this book, by my positive belief's. As for where I'm going from here—it's my desire and passion to continue to help those who are struggling with their own adversities and to guide them to see there is always *hope* within them if only they believe.

Sometimes the bad things that happen in our lives, put us directly on the path to the best things that will ever happen to us …

Lightning Source UK Ltd.
Milton Keynes UK
UKHW041602301218
334668UK00001B/30/P